Linspired

Other books in the
Zonderkidz Biography Series:

Linspired

the
Jeremy Lin
Story

**Mike Yorkey
with Jesse Florea**

ZONDERVAN.com/
AUTHORTRACKER
follow your favorite authors

ZONDERKIDZ

Linspired
Copyright © 2013 by Mike Yorkey and Jesse Florea

This title is also available as a Zondervan ebook.
Visit www.zondervan.com/ebooks

Requests for information should be addressed to:
Zonderkidz, 5300 Patterson Ave SE, Grand Rapids, Michigan 49530

ISBN: 978-0-310-742883

Portions of *Linspired* previously appeared in *Playing with Purpose: Inside the Lives and Faith of Top NBA Stars* by Mike Yorkey and are used by permission. *Linspired* is based on research and interviews with Jeremy Lin but has not been authorized by him.

Cover design: Kris Nelson
Interior composition: Greg Johnson/TextbookPerfect

Printed in the United States

13 14 15 16 17 18 19 20 /DCI/ 22 21 20 19 18 17 16 15 14 13 12 11 10 9 8 7 6 5 4 3 2 1

Table of Contents

Chapter 1

The NBA Goes Linsane!

Seven, Six, Five, Four ...

Any child who has picked up a basketball dreams of one day hitting a game-winning, buzzer-beating shot. Jeremy Lin grew up with images of hoops glory running through his mind as he dribbled a basketball on his family's driveway in Palo Alto, California. He'd shoot for hours, counting down from ten and releasing the ball just before the buzzer sounded. Sometimes Jeremy's shot would rip through the net with a beautiful *swish*. Other attempts would bounce off the rim and fall disappointingly to the pavement.

On those occasions, Jeremy would gather the ball, take his place on the driveway, and start the countdown again. His team just had to win.

Seven, Six, Five, Four ...

Even with all of Jeremy's practice and dreaming, he never would have dared to imagine what took place on February 14, 2012.

Through a bizarre series of what can only be explained as God-ordained events, the twenty-three-year-old found himself starting as point guard for the New York Knicks. Just weeks before, Jeremy feared he'd be cut by his third NBA team in two years. Now in a game against the Toronto Raptors, Jeremy held the ball at half court as the clock ticked down from eighteen seconds.

"Tied at eighty-seven, Lin with the ball in his hands," the TSN announcer said as the crowd at Air Canada Center rose to its feet. Jeremy had helped erase a 17-point second-half deficit for the Knicks. Moments earlier his three-point play on a double-pump, feathery four-foot jumper and ensuing foul shot had knotted the game 87–87.

With five seconds to go, Jeremy started dribbling toward Toronto point guard Jose Calderon. Jeremy moved the ball between his legs, spotted up about twenty-four feet from the basket, and launched a high-arching three-pointer.

Three, Two . . .

"Lin for the *wiiin*," the announcer shouted. "Got it!"

The crowd erupted as the ball swished through the hoop, giving the Knicks a 90–87 victory. Jeremy nodded his head triumphantly and backpedaled down the court before getting chest-pumped by teammates pouring off the Knicks' bench. With that shot, Jeremy clinched New York's sixth straight victory and took the worldwide "Linsanity" craze to another level.

The NBA Goes Linsane!

Frank Gunn/The Canadian Press/AP Images

After his long jumper was the difference in the Knicks' 90-87 victory over the Toronto Raptors on February 14, 2012, a joyful Jeremy points heavenward. Notice his wristband, which reads "In Jesus' Name I Play."

"I'm just glad it went like this so we can calm the Linsanity down," Knicks' coach Mike D'Antoni joked after the game.[1]

Even though the Knicks were playing a road game, the crowd's reaction seemed more fitting for New York's Madison Square Garden. The hometown Raptors had lost, but the crowd stayed on its feet, cheering for the NBA's newest hero. Jeremy's box score on the night: 27 points (12 of which came in the fourth quarter) and 11 assists. Toronto fans, just like basketball fans around the world, were caught up in a wave of excitement surrounding a player who quickly came to embody hard work, hustle, and a rock solid faith in God.

But what some people missed on that February evening was the fact that D'Antoni chose not to take a timeout when New York got possession of the ball with less than twenty-four seconds left and the score tied. Conventional wisdom in the NBA says to call a timeout, draw up a play, and make sure the right players are on the court. Instead the coach put the ball in Jeremy's hands and trusted him with the outcome.

"He's too good to call a timeout," D'Antoni said to reporters after the game. "It makes it easy to a coach to be able to trust your point guard. He's smart enough, and I have faith in him."[2]

No, D'Antoni wasn't talking about Carmelo Anthony — perhaps the Knicks' most clutch performer, who missed the game with an injury. The coach's words weren't directed toward a wily veteran player who'd been in last-second situations hundreds of times. And he wasn't even describing a top-five NBA draft pick who was destined for basketball stardom since middle school. He was talking about Jeremy Lin—who was five feet, three inches *in high school*, failed to get drafted by any NBA team, and was making just his fifth start.

Obviously, Linsanity wasn't just sweeping the world; it was affecting his coach too.

In early February 2012, Jeremy was the last man coming off the Knicks' bench during garbage time; by Valentine's Day, his dribble drive through five Los Angeles Lakers graced the cover of *Sports Illustrated,* basketball pundits on ESPN's *SportsCenter* had run out of superlatives to describe him, and his number 17 Knicks jersey was the NBA's top seller.

He was called "Lincredible," a balm of "Liniment" for the NBA. And he moved from anonymity to stardom—even pop icon status—quicker than an outlet pass to start a fast break.

Nobody was saying that Jeremy was the next Steve Nash, Magic Johnson, or Jerry West, but the fact that Jeremy even made it onto an NBA roster was noteworthy for several reasons:

1. At 6 feet, 3 inches, he wasn't tall for a game dominated by humongous athletes who can jump out of the gym.

2. He came from an Ivy League school; Harvard University, which last sent a player to the NBA in 1953—the year *before* the league adopted a 24-second shot clock.

3. He was the first American-born player of Chinese or Taiwanese descent to ever play in the NBA.

The uniqueness of his story—his racial background, his Ivy League pedigree, and his undrafted status—caught the world's attention. But there was more to Jeremy—a deep reservoir of faith. Here was a polite, humble, and hard-working young man who understood that God had a purpose for his life, whatever that might be.

Jeremy sees himself as a Christian first and a basketball player second. In the midst of his wild, implausible journey with a leather basketball in his hands—he was trusting God.

"I'm not exactly sure how it is all going to turn out," Jeremy had said after his rookie season, "but I know for a fact that God has called me to be here now in the NBA. And this is the assignment that he has given me. I know I wouldn't be here if that wasn't the case. Just looking back, though, it's been a huge miracle [that I'm in the NBA]. I can see his fingerprints everywhere."

God's hand was certainly guiding Jeremy during his first handful of starts for the Knicks, where the young point guard accomplished something that not even Michael Jordan—Jeremy's childhood hero—could brag about.

Who's Responsible for the Linsanity?

On February 13, 2012, Jeremy Lin filed an application with the U.S. Patent and Trademark Office to own the term "Linsanity." His filing came six days after a thirty-five-year-old Californian applied for a Linsanity trademark.

Despite not being the first to apply, Gary Krugman, a partner at the Washington-based law firm of Sughrue Mion, said Jeremy's claim should trump the others.

"Nobody can register a mark if it falsely suggests a connection with the person or an institution," Krugman said. "I would guess that Jeremy Lin would be able to oppose on the grounds that Linsanity points uniquely and unmistakably to him."[3]

If you haven't seen them already, don't be surprised to find Linsanity bags, cups, T-shirts, and other products in a sporting goods store near you.

Chapter 2

Miracle Near 34th Street

What do Michael Jordan, Magic Johnson, LeBron James, Dirk Nowitzki, Kevin Durant, and Kobe Bryant all have in common? None of them scored more points or dished out more assists than Jeremy did in his first five NBA starts.

In fact, no player in recorded NBA history (statistics started to be kept when the NBA and ABA merged in 1976) had scored at least twenty points and tallied seven assists in each of his first five starts at basketball's highest level. Jeremy's scoring prowess also set an NBA record, as his 136 points were the most ever for a player's first five games as a starter.

In one short week—just a handful of games in a lockout-shortened season—Jeremy progressed from benchwarmer to the toast of the Big Apple as the Knicks' leading scorer, playmaker, and spiritual leader.

West of the Hudson River, he became the focus of a normally fragmented media universe and set the 24/7 social networking world on fire. Everybody was talking about Jeremy: sports talk shows, blog writers, TV shows, even late night talk show hosts and sketch comedy programs. Trying to figure out how many smartphones, laptops, and computers converged to create a tidal wave of tweets, touts, and online chatter would make your head spin faster than Jeremy's spin move to the basket.

The reason Linsanity went viral was simple: everyone loves an underdog story, and his improbable journey has all the ingredients of a Hollywood fairy tale.

Trailblazing Asian-American in the NBA.

Harvard grad.

Cut by two teams and riding the bench in New York.

Even the fact that he had been sleeping on his older brother Josh's couch on the Lower East Side of Manhattan was part of the lore. People imagined the poor guy huddled under a blanket in Josh's living room because there was no room at the inn.

More important to Jeremy than his personal statistics was the fact that New York started to win. Before Jeremy was inserted into the lineup, New York had lost eleven of thirteen games and sat near the bottom of the Atlantic division with an 8–15 record. All-star Carmelo Anthony sat out with an injury. And high-scoring forward Amar'e Stoudemire was with his family after the death of his brother. Even coach Mike D'Antoni had his job on the line as the proud Knicks franchise wasn't living up to expectations. (D'Antoni did end up stepping down as head coach on March 14.)

Then during a February 4, 2012, game against the New Jersey Nets, Carmelo encouraged D'Antoni to play Jeremy in the second half. After all, things couldn't get worse. Melo had competed against Jeremy in practice and appreciated his spunk and hustle.

Jeremy made the most of the opportunity by scoring 25 points to lead New York to a come-from-behind 99-92 victory. Over the next twelve games, the Knicks went 9-3 to even their record at 18-18 and get themselves back into the playoff picture.

"They're playing at a high level," Boston Celtics all-star Kevin Garnett said. "Lin is obviously taking over the world. That's dope. You always like to see someone succeed at what they love. He plays with a lot of passion, and he's [giving] them, not just the city, but that team—life."[1]

Jeremy's passion showed as he dove for balls on the hardwood, drove into the lane against bigger and stronger players, and even shouted at teammates to keep pushing themselves.

Sometimes Jeremy's zest for the game got him in trouble. Not only did he score more points in his first five starts than any player in NBA history, he also committed a record number of turnovers. Jeremy averaged more than five turnovers a game, which isn't the kind of statistic point guards brag about.

Of course, there *are* different kinds of turnovers. Some players turn over the ball by making a weak pass or playing timidly. Jeremy's turnovers often resulted from his aggressive play in driving to the basket or trying to thread a pass to a teammate under the hoop. Those kinds of turnovers are much easier for a coach to forgive. Plus, Jeremy's aggressive play and excellent court vision frequently resulted in monster dunks or wide-open three-pointers for fellow Knicks.

"He can really create for himself and his teammates," Hall of Fame point guard Magic Johnson said about Jeremy. "That's why Knicks fans are enjoying basketball, because they now have an exciting team."[2]

Perhaps no player benefited more from Jeremy's presence on the court than fifth-year pro Steve Novak. Steve, like Jeremy, played limited minutes for the Knicks before the month of February. The excellent long-range shooter immediately gelled with the slashing point guard. Steve often couldn't create an open shot for himself, but with Jeremy collapsing defenses with his forays to the basket, Steve routinely found himself left alone and on the receiving end of a pass from Jeremy. Steve connected on nearly 50 percent of his three-point shots once Jeremy started playing and averaged nearly 12 points a game (which is much better than his career 3.6 point scoring average).

Jeremy's story became the feel-good hit of the 2012 season as he energized New York and revitalized his basketball dreams. Of course, none of this could've been possible if his parents hadn't come to the United States to chase their American dream.

Seeing Double

Jeremy Lin must have felt on top of the world when his photo appeared on the cover of *Sports Illustrated* on February 20, 2012. But a week later, he was floating *above* the clouds. On February 27, Jeremy's picture graced the covers of *Sports Illustrated* and *Time* — two of the biggest magazines in the United States. By making the cover of *SI* twice in a row, Jeremy joined Michael Jordan and Dirk Nowitzki as the only NBA players to earn this honor.

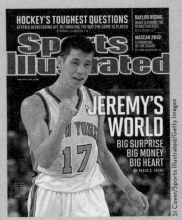

How rare is that double? Since 1990, only eleven other athletes have graced the cover of *Sports Illustrated*, the country's premier sports magazine, for two consecutive weeks.

Chapter 3

Coming to America

Jeremy's story begins in an unlikely place: war-torn China in the late 1940s. Civil war had ripped apart the world's most populous country. Chinese Nationalist forces led by General Chiang Kai-shek fought the People's Liberation Army—led by Chinese Communist Party leader Mao Zedong—for control of China. At that time, a small elite class of Chinese lived well, while hundreds of millions barely survived. In 1949, after three years of bloody conflict, the Communist forces won. Chiang Kai-shek and approximately two million Nationalist Chinese fled for their lives to the island of Taiwan. Among those refugees were Jeremy's grandparents on his mother's side.

Jeremy's mother, Shirley (Shirley is actually an anglicized version of her Chinese first name), was born in Taiwan. Her mother (Jeremy's grandmother) was one of

Taiwan's first prominent female physicians. During the 1970s, some American doctors visited Taiwan to study the advances Taiwanese physicians had made in health care. As Shirley's mother connected with the American medical community, a seed was planted to immigrate to the United States, where the family could pursue a better life. In 1978, just after Shirley graduated from high school, her family moved to the United States.

Shirley worked hard learning English and soon enrolled at Old Dominion University, a college in Norfolk, Virginia. She majored in computer science, a field with a bright future. Experts felt a computer revolution would explode in the 1980s, because a newfangled invention called the personal computer had begun finding its way into American homes.

There weren't too many Asians (or second-generation Asian-Americans, for that matter) at Old Dominion. The dozen or so Chinese-speaking students formed a small Asian support group for fun and fellowship. One member of the group was a graduate student from Taiwan — a handsome young man named Gie-Ming Lin, who'd come to the United States to work on his doctorate in computer engineering. His ancestors had lived in Taiwan since the nineteenth century, long before Communist oppression began on China's mainland.

Sharing the same cultural background and a common language brought Gie-Ming and Shirley together, and they began dating. Not long after, a love blossomed. When Gie-Ming told Shirley of his plan to finish his doctorate at Purdue University in West Lafayette, Indiana, she

Handout/Reuters/Landov

Lin Chu A-muen, the mother of Gie-Ming, came over from Taiwan to help raise the family during Jeremy's formative years.

decided to transfer to Purdue and continue her under-graduate classes in computer science.

While at Purdue, Shirley attended a Christian fellowship group and heard about Jesus Christ's love and sacrifice for her. Curious about who Jesus was, she explored and learned about the Lord of the universe and how he came to Earth to die for her sins. She prayed to accept Christ's gift of forgiveness and committed to follow Jesus. When she told Gie-Ming what she had done, he investigated the gospel and prayed to become a Christian as well. They soon plugged into a Chinese-speaking church and began their walk with Christ.

Gie-Ming and Shirley married while they were still in school. They liked living in the United States and became two of the many millions of immigrants chasing the American dream.

They certainly weren't afraid to work hard—or live frugally. Early on, Gie-Ming and Shirley would go fishing on weekends at a nearby reservoir. Gie-Ming, who loved fishing and was quite good at it, would catch his limit of bluegill, shad, crappie, or bass and bring home his haul in a galvanized bucket. They would dine on fish that night and toss the rest into the freezer to eat during the week.

One evening, Gie-Ming flipped on the television to relax and came across a basketball game. The Lakers were playing the Celtics during one of their great 1980s NBA Finals battles. The sight of Larry Bird and Magic Johnson doing wondrous things on Boston Garden's parquet floor mesmerized Gie-Ming. He was smitten by the athleticism of these larger-than-life figures who made the basketball court look small. Gie-Ming started watching NBA basketball every chance he had, which wasn't often since his studies and part-time work took up much of his free time.

Wait! A new technology had arrived in people's homes during that time. It was called a VHS recorder. This then state-of-the-art electromechanical device could record television broadcasts on cassettes that contained magnetic tape. Suddenly, the images and sound of TV shows and sporting events could be played back at a more convenient time—or replayed over and over

Handout/Reuters/Landov

One-year-old Jeremy is held in the arms of his father, Gie-Ming, on this outing with his older brother, Josh, and his grandmother, Lin Chu A-muen.

for the viewer's enjoyment. The advent of the VHS recorder revolutionized the way Gie-Ming—and millions of Americans—watched TV in the 1980s.

Gie-Ming started taping NBA games. He loved watching Kareem Abdul Jabbar's sky hook, Julius "Dr. J" Erving's gravity-defying dunks, and Magic leading the fast break and handling a basketball like it was on the end of a string. Gie-Ming soon became a certifiable basketball junkie. He studied those tapes with the same fervor as when he studied for his Ph.D. He couldn't tell friends *why* he loved basketball, he just did.

Gie-Ming also started playing a bit of basketball. He taught himself how to dribble and shoot by practicing at a nearby playground. He was too shy to join a basketball league, but he occasionally played a pickup game. He loved breaking a sweat on the basketball court, which became his favorite form of exercise.

When Gie-Ming and Shirley completed their schooling at Purdue, they moved to Los Angeles, where Gie-Ming worked for a company that designed microchips. Shirley jumped on the mommy track and gave birth to their first child, a son they named Joshua. Two years later, on August 23, 1988, ten years to the day after Kobe Bryant entered the world, Jeremy Shu-How Lin was born. And it didn't take long before he had a basketball in his hands.

Lin-credible Taiwan

Taiwan sits about 140 miles from mainland China. Although Taiwan is the same size as Maryland and Delaware combined, nearly twenty-three million people live in this island nation. (That's four times more than live in Delaware and Maryland.)

With both of Jeremy Lin's parents being born in Taiwan, Linsanity hit even harder there than even in the U.S. There were days where Jeremy's photo appeared on the front page of all four Taiwanese newspapers. Basketball courts in schools and parks were quickly fixed up as more children caught basketball fever. Xinbei High School even took a break from classes so its 4,000 students could watch Jeremy on TV. They clapped red noisemakers and jumped up and down as Jeremy raced around the hardwood.

"The students pleaded and I agreed to do this on an experimental basis," principal Wang Chi-kuang said.[1]

But after the game, it was back to the books. Students take their studies very seriously in Taiwan.

Taiwanese fans gather at a Taipei sports bar to watch Jeremy and the Knicks play during Linsanity. Many Americans don't realize how popular Jeremy is in the Asian culture, who see him as one of their own.

Chapter 4

Hoop and Faith

In the early 1990s, Silicon Valley lured Jeremy's parents to Northern California. Gie-Ming's expertise became computer chip design, while Shirley—who had given birth to her third son, Joseph—returned to work in her specialty quality control, which meant she made sure new computer programs were bug-free when they released.

The Lins settled in Palo Alto, a community of sixty thousand residents that bordered Stanford University. Gie-Ming, who wanted to introduce his favorite game— basketball—to his three sons, signed up for a family membership at the local YMCA. When firstborn Joshua was five years old, Gie-Ming showed him the fundamentals of basketball by using the passing, dribbling, and shooting drills he'd studied on his VHS tapes. Jeremy received the same instruction when he started kindergarten, and so would Joseph when he reached that age.

When Jeremy entered first grade, his parents put him in a youth basketball league. But at that age, Jeremy wasn't interested in the action on the court. He was like those kids in T-ball who lay down on the outfield grass and watch the clouds pass by instead of paying attention to the next batter. Most of the time, Jeremy stood at halfcourt and sucked his thumb while the ball went up and down the floor. Since he couldn't be coaxed to try harder, his mom stopped coming to the games.

As Jeremy matured, he became more interested in basketball, especially after he grew big enough to launch an effective shot toward the rim and watch it swish through the net. As shot after shot poured through the hoop, he was hooked. He asked his mother if she would come back and watch him play, but she wanted to know if he was actually going to try before she committed to returning to his games.

"You watch," he promised. "I'm going to play, and I'm going to score."

He scored all right. Sometimes Jeremy scored the maximum amount of points one player was allowed under the league's rules.

For the rest of Jeremy's elementary school years, his parents regularly took him and his brothers to the gym to play basketball. They also enrolled Jeremy in youth soccer, but basketball was his passion.

As the demands of schoolwork grew, Jeremy and his brothers would do their homework after school, wait for their father to come home for dinner, and then everyone would head over to the Y at eight o'clock for ninety minutes of shooting and pickup games. Gie-Ming continued to stress the fundamentals because he wanted the game's basic moves to become second nature to Jeremy and his brothers.

As Jeremy improved, he couldn't get enough hoops action. On many nights, he and his family practiced and played right up until they closed the doors at the Palo Alto Family YMCA at 9:45 p.m.

While basketball turned out to be a fun family sport for the Lins, they weren't going to sacrifice academics or church on the altar of basketball. Academics were important to Gie-Ming and Shirley because they had seen firsthand how education could provide a better life. Church was even more important because they knew what a relationship with Christ meant to them and to the spiritual well-being of their sons.

Wherever they lived, the Lins gravitated toward Chinese Christian churches. When they moved to Palo Alto, they found a church they immediately liked: the Chinese Church in Christ in nearby Mountain View. This place of worship was really two churches in one. Every Sunday morning there were services — in Mandarin and in English — in separate fellowship halls. (The Mandarin-speaking services were actually better attended than the ones presented in English.)

The strong demand for a church service in Mandarin was reflective of the demographics of the San Francisco Bay Area, home to the nation's highest concentration of Asian-Americans. At one time, the U.S. Census revealed that 27 percent of the people living in Palo

Alto were Asian-Americans — racially identifying themselves as Chinese-American, Filipino-American, Korean-American, Japanese-American, or Vietnamese-American. There was a large Taiwanese-American community in nearby Cupertino (24 percent of the population), while other communities like Millbrae, Foster City, Piedmont, and Albany had Asian populations of 10 percent or greater.

Stephen Chen, pastor of the Chinese Church in Christ's Redeemer Bible Fellowship, remembers the first time he met Jeremy in 2001, when Stephen was a twenty-three-year-old youth counselor.

"Jeremy was around thirteen when I first ran into him," he said. "We were having a church cleaning day, and he was running around with his friends and being rambunctious. I remember scolding him, saying, 'Hey, we're trying to clean things up, and you're making things more messy.'"

Feeling chastised, Jeremy went home and told his parents he didn't want to go to that church anymore because the youth guy had been mean to him. His parents didn't take his side, however, and the incident soon blew over.

Stephen, who was looking for things to do with the youth group, discovered that Jeremy and his older brother, Josh, were avid basketball players. Josh was starting to play on the high school team, while Jeremy was living and breathing the game in junior high.

"I hadn't played a lick of basketball before that time," Stephen said. "But I wanted to connect with the Lin brothers, so I asked them if we could do a little exchange:

I would teach them about the Bible and they would teach me how to play basketball."

Josh and Jeremy readily accepted. After youth group was over, they'd go to a nearby basketball court, where the Lin brothers taught Stephen how to do a layup, properly shoot the ball, and box out on rebounds. Then they would get the youth group together, choose up sides, and play games.

"Jeremy would pass me the ball, even when the game was on the line," Stephen said. "He wasn't afraid that I'd lose the game. If we did lose, his older brother would get upset, but Jeremy would even console his brother. Even at that young age, Jeremy was hospitable, eager to get along with different types of people. He was also a natural leader, and kids listened to him."

Before entering high school, Jeremy wanted to get baptized as a public statement that he believed in Jesus Christ as his Lord and Savior. The Chinese Church in Christ had a baptismal inside the church sanctuary, and Jeremy was dunked during a Sunday morning service. Not long after that, Stephen asked him if he'd become part of the youth ministry's leadership team.

Jeremy accepted. The church had been renting out a local high school gym on Sunday evenings so the kids in the youth group could play basketball and invite their friends to join them. "Jeremy would always be the one who would ask other kids to come out and play basketball with us," Stephen said. "And they would come. Jeremy wanted everyone to feel at home. That was just another way he extended kindness to others."

The gym had two full courts. Many dads saw how much fun their kids were having, so they would play too — fathers on one court and their sons on the other. Moms would often visit with each other during the games.

All this basketball playing — after school, on weekends, and on Sunday nights — helped Jeremy to become quite a player. Even though he was a shrimp on the court, he caught the eye of Palo Alto High School coach Peter Diepenbrock, who met Jeremy when he was in fifth grade at a summer basketball camp.

"He was very, very small," the coach remembered. "But a very good player — very good instincts, very good feel — and his leadership stuck out. He just has an extremely strong will, and he exerts his will on every game that he's in."[1]

Diepenbrock continued to watch Jeremy progress. The coach knew Jeremy was the best junior high player, but he had concerns about his size.

As Jeremy entered his freshman year of high school, he topped out at five feet, three inches tall and weighed 125 pounds. Jeremy had set his sights on playing high school basketball, but he knew that if he didn't grow a lot in the next couple of years, he wasn't going to get a chance to play — no matter how talented he was.

One day, Jeremy told Stephen, "I want to be at least six feet tall."

Stephen looked at Jeremy. He knew the stereotype of Asians being short, and there was some truth to that. The average male height in the United States is five feet, ten inches, while in China, the average male height is five feet, seven inches. Unfortunately for Jeremy, his parents weren't tall either. Both stood five feet, six inches, so he didn't have a great gene pool working for him.

"How are you going to become six feet tall?" Stephen asked.

"I'm going to drink milk every day," young Jeremy replied.

For the next few years, Shirley made constant trips the local supermarket to buy milk by the gallon. Jeremy drank the dairy product like it was ... water. He had a glass of milk with his breakfast cereal, drank milk at lunch, and always had a couple of more glasses of milk with dinner. He also gulped calcium supplements like they were candy.

"I drank so much milk because I was obsessed with my height," Jeremy said. "I'd wake up in the morning and measure myself every day because I heard that you're always taller in the morning, at least when you're growing. I wanted to see if I had grown overnight."

Jeremy's greatest wish was to be taller than his older brother, Josh, who was in the midst of a growth spurt that took him to five feet, ten inches in high school. Desperate to will his body to grow taller, Jeremy even climbed the monkey bars at school and let himself hang upside down, thinking it would extend his spinal column and make him taller.

Jeremy understood that he couldn't "force" his body to grow, but he also believed that to be competitive in the game of basketball, he had to grow to at least six feet.

And that was a tall order.

Band for Christian Brothers

Jeremy doesn't make a bold statement on the court with flashy tattoos or a crazy hairdo. But the orange wristbands that he sports on both wrists carry a bold message: In Jesus' Name I Play. A Christian company called Active Faith, started by former NBA player Lanny Smith and Minnesota Timberwolves forward Anthony Tolliver, manufactures the wristbands, which cost $3. A former D-League teammate, Patrick Ewing Jr., introduced Jeremy to Active Faith.

Chapter 5

Miracle Grow

When Jeremy moved up to Palo Alto High School, he made a big impression on his freshman basketball coach—even though he was one of the smallest players on the team. Years of playing in YMCA youth basketball leagues had honed his skills. His freshman coach stood up at the team's end-of-the-season banquet and declared, "Jeremy has a better skill set than anyone I've seen at his age."[1]

And then something miraculous happened.

Jeremy grew.

And grew.

And grew.

By his junior year, he had sprouted *nine inches* to reach the magic number—six feet. He was still as skinny as a beanstalk, weighing around a buck-fifty. Call it answered prayer or milk doing his body good, but Jeremy went on to add two more inches of height by his senior

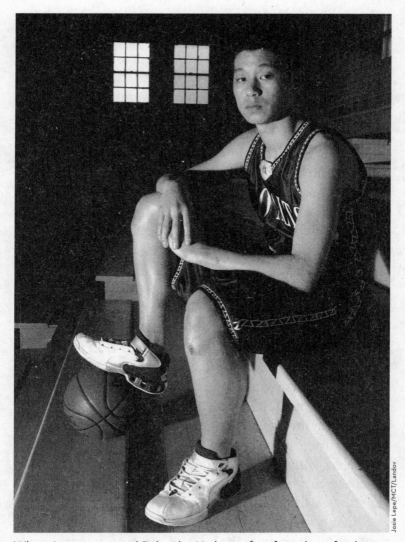

Josie Lepe/MCT/Landov

When Jeremy entered Palo Alto High as a five-foot-three freshman, his goal was to reach six feet in height so he would be a competitive basketball player.

year of high school to reach six feet, two inches. (Jeremy turned out to be a real late bloomer: he added *another* inch and a half during his college years to reach his present height, which is a tad over six feet, three inches. He also added strength by hitting the weight room in college, ending up at a solid 200 pounds.)

No longer the shortest player on the court, Jeremy showed his coaches and Palo Alto High opponents that he could run the offense, shoot lights-out, and play tough defense. His position, point guard, may be the most specialized role in basketball. The point guard leads the team's half-court offense, runs the fast break, makes the right pass at the right time, works the pick-and-roll, and penetrates the defense to create for open teammates when he gets double-teamed.

When Jeremy dribbled the ball into the front court, he thought like a quarterback approaching the line of scrimmage and scanning the defense to find its vulnerabilities. Jeremy's mind quickly determined how an opponent's defense was set up and where the weak spots were. Then his quickness would make defenses pay for their shortcomings.

His father, always ahead of the technological curve, had been filming Jeremy since his junior high days. After the games, father and son would review what happened, gleaning ways to improve from the tapes.

During his sophomore year, Jeremy was not only good enough to win the role of starting varsity point guard, but his fantastic play also earned him the first of three first-team All-Santa Clara Valley Athletic League

Dai Sugano/MCT/Landov

With a quick first step; Jeremy drives past a defender in this high school basketball game. Jeremy led Palo Alto High to a California state championship his senior year.

awards. His junior season was even better. Jeremy was the driving force behind Palo Alto High, helping the team set a school record for victories by posting a 32–2 record.

His coach, Peter Diepenbrock, recognized that he had something special and turned Jeremy loose. He sat down his point guard and said, "Let's tell it like it is. I'm the defensive coordinator; you're the offensive coordinator. Just get it done."[2]

And that's what Jeremy did his senior year when he propelled his team to the Division II California state championship. Even before the season started, Jeremy stood up and said his goal for the team was to win a state title.

"I was like, *No way. That's not going to happen,*" Vikings teammate Kevin Trimble remembered thinking. "But we did it."[3]

Going into the championship game, Palo Alto was a huge underdog against perennial powerhouse Mater Dei, a Catholic high school from Southern California. No team had won more state basketball titles than Mater Dei, and the Monarchs, who had a 32–2 record, came into the game ranked among the nation's top teams.

Talk about a David-versus-Goliath matchup. Mater Dei was loaded with Division I recruits and had eight players six feet, seven inches or taller. Palo Alto had no one over six feet, six inches. Playing at Arco Arena, home of the Sacramento Kings, Jeremy flew all over the court to personally engineer the plucky and undersized Palo Alto team to a two-point lead with two minutes to play. But could the Vikings hang on?

Jeremy brought the ball up the floor, trying to eat up as much clock as possible. Suddenly, there were just seconds left on the 35-second shot clock. Jeremy, still well above the top of the key, decided to launch a rainbow toward the rim to beat the shot-clock buzzer. The ball banked in, giving Palo Alto a five-point lead.

Mater Dei wasn't finished yet, and neither was Jeremy. The Monarchs cut the lead to two points with thirty seconds to go. Jeremy dribbled the ball into the front court. Mater Dei didn't want to foul him, because the Monarchs knew he was an excellent free throw shooter, so they waited for him to pass to a teammate. Jeremy, however, sensed an opening and drove to the basket in a flash, taking on Mater Dei's star player, six-foot, eight-inch Taylor King. Jeremy went up and over Taylor for a layup that gave him a total of 17 points in the game and iced a 51–47 state championship victory.

"There are guys that are terrific players, but when the stage gets big, they shrink," said Jim Sutter, Jeremy's AAU coach for five years. "For Jeremy, it's always been that he glows—he just glows—when he's in the spotlight. It's just his makeup. It's his determination to succeed."[4]

You'd think that with all the college scouts in the stands for a state championship game, Jeremy would have been barraged with offers to play at the next level. But the recruiting interest had been underwhelming all season long and stayed that way even after the win over Mater Dei. It wasn't like Jeremy played for a tumbleweed-strewn high school in the middle of the Nevada desert. He was part of a respected program at Palo Alto High, and coach Diepenbrock was well known to college coaches.

What's more, Jeremy was highly regarded in Northern California high school basketball circles. He earned first-team All-State and Northern California's Division II

Scholar Athlete of the Year honors. The *San Francisco Chronicle* newspaper named him Boys Player of the Year, as did the *San Jose Mercury News* and the *Palo Alto Daily News.*

Despite all the great ink and a bushel basket of post-season awards, despite sending out numerous DVD highlights that a friend at church had prepared, and despite Coach Diepenbrock's lobbying efforts with college coaches, Jeremy did not receive *any* scholarship offers to play Division I basketball. Not even from Stanford University, which was located literally across the street from Palo Alto High. (A wide boulevard named El Camino Real separates the two schools.)

It's perplexing why Stanford didn't offer Jeremy a scholarship. After all, Jeremy had the background that the Cardinals look for in their student-athletes:

- great high school basketball résumé
- local product
- strong academic record
- Asian-American

Regarding the last bullet point, almost 20 percent of the undergraduate student body at Stanford was Asian-American. But the Stanford basketball program took a pass. Some Stanford boosters interceded for Jeremy, telling the coaches that they had to give this Lin kid a look. But the best response the family received was that Jeremy could try to make the team as a walk-on.

The Lins' eyes turned across the bay toward Berkeley, but the University of California coaching staff said the same thing: *You can try to walk on, but no guarantees.* During one recruiting visit, a Cal coach accidentally called Jeremy "Ron," something that almost never happens with blue-chip recruits.

The disrespect continued at Jeremy's dream school — UCLA, where Josh was enrolled. Jeremy would have loved to play for the storied Bruins program, and he was the kind of upstanding young man legendary Bruin coach John Wooden would have recruited back in the 1960s and 1970s. But the message from UCLA coaches was the same: *You'll have to make the team as a walk-on.*

Jeremy knew that few walk-ons — non-scholarship players invited to try out for the team — ever stick on a Division I basketball roster. He would never say it himself, but some basketball observers thought the fact that Jeremy *was* Asian-American cost him a Division I scholarship. Recruiters couldn't look past his ethnicity, couldn't imagine an Asian-looking kid having the game to compete against the very best players in the country. For whatever reason, they couldn't picture him playing basketball at the Division I level, so Jeremy turned his sights to the opposite coast.

Taking It Nice and Easy

Jeremy fearlessly pushed the ball up the court while playing for the Palo Alto High basketball team, but he was more cautious on the road as he took his driver's license test. He flunked his first time because he drove too slow — 15 mph in a 25 mph residential zone.

Chapter 6

It's Academic

Jeremy had run into a "system" that blocked his path to a Division I basketball program like two Shaquille O'Neal-like centers blocking the way to the basket. College coaches, who are the decision makers, look for something quantifiable in a high school player—like how tall he is, how high he can jump, or how many points per game he scores. Jeremy's greatest strengths didn't show up in a box score.

"His strength is really hard to quantify," said his high school coach, Peter Diepenbrock. "It's not like he's six feet, five inches, or a pure shooter, or a really great ball handler. What he is really about is winning and understanding the game."[1]

His game was running the show, leading the offense, and setting up teammates. He had an incredible feel on the court, a Magic Johnson-like peripheral vision, and a take-charge attitude that coaches love to see in their point guards.

"He knew exactly what needed to be done at every point in the basketball game," Coach Diepenbrock said. "He was able to exert his will on basketball games in ways you would not expect. It was just hard to quantify his fearlessness."[2]

The problem likely stemmed from the fact that major college coaches had never recruited a standout Asian player before, so they didn't know what to do with Jeremy. Asian-American gym rats like him were a novelty in college basketball; only one out of every two hundred Division I basketball players came from Asian-American households. In many coaches' minds, college basketball stars looked different than Jeremy.

The Lins had some options, however, thanks to Gie-Ming's and Shirley's insistence that their sons study and perform just as well in the classroom as they did on the basketball court. Shirley was a bit of a no-nonsense taskmaster who made sure Jeremy put as much effort into his schoolbooks as he did into improving his jump shot.

And Shirley was willing to work hard too. During her son's high school career, she volunteered as team mom — organizing rides to games, booking hotel reservations, ordering flowers for senior night, and even compiling statistics of upcoming opponents. Shirley also kept close watch on all three of her boys as he worked at Sun Microsystems.

One time, Coach Diepenbrock picked up a phone call from Shirley, who had some distressing news: Jeremy's grade in a math class had slipped to a precarious A-. "Peter, Peter, Jeremy has an A- in this class. If it's not an A by next week, I am taking him off basketball," she threatened.[3]

"Yes, I will stay on top of Jeremy," the coach promised.

Thankfully, Jeremy righted his academic ship. Throughout high school, he carried a 4.2 grade-point average (in Palo Alto High's grade-point system, an A was worth 4 points, but AP, or Advanced Placement classes, were weighted heavier because of their difficulty) and even scored a perfect 800 on his SAT II Math 2C test during his *freshman* year. Jeremy's parents felt that if Pac-10 and other Division I teams didn't want their son, then maybe he could play for a top-ranked academic college—like Harvard.

The Lins looked east—toward the eight Ivy League schools, which are the most selective (and therefore elite) universities in the United States. Harvard and Brown each stepped up; both coaches said they'd guarantee Jeremy a roster spot. Each made the case that they *really* wanted him to play for their basketball programs.

In the Lin family, there was no discussion. If Harvard— the assumed number 1 school in the country in nearly everyone's eyes—wanted him, then he was going to play basketball for the Crimson, even if it meant they would pay for his schooling out of their own pockets. Harvard, like Yale, Princeton, Columbia, and the rest of the Ivy League schools, doesn't offer athletic scholarships.

This was no small consideration for Jeremy's parents. In round numbers, a year of undergraduate studies at

Harvard cost fifty thousand dollars, which covered tuition, room and board, books, fees, and other expenses. The Lins were already shelling out for Josh's education at UCLA.

"The tuition is nuts," Jeremy said. "My parents did everything they could to get me through school. I received some financial aid from Harvard and took some loans out. But I wouldn't have [gotten accepted by Harvard] if they hadn't been pushing me."

Good thing that Gie-Ming and Shirley kept their eyes on the academic ball. Harvard not only turned out to be a great basketball school for Jeremy—where his game could grow—but a place that added to the Jeremy Lin legend.

By the Numbers

18: The number of Asian-American men's players in Division I college basketball (0.4 percent) when Jeremy Lin played at Harvard. (Source: The 2009 NCAA Race and Ethnicity Report)

23: The number of students at Harvard with the last name of Lin while Jeremy attended the school.

Chapter 7

Raising the Curtain on the Jeremy Lin Show

Harvard basketball began at the turn of the 20th century. In 1900, John Kirkland Clark, a Harvard Law School student, introduced the game to the university just eight years after Dr. James Naismith invented the game at a YMCA Training School in Springfield, Massachusetts.

Despite being located just eighty-eight miles from basketball's birthplace, Harvard didn't have much to show for 106 years of basketball tradition by the time Jeremy arrived on campus in the fall of 2006. The Crimson had *never* won an Ivy League conference title and had not qualified for the NCAA tournament since 1946. (Harvard finally earned a March Madness bid again in 2012.) In four seasons prior to Jeremy's arrival, Harvard's record was 43-65. Winning seasons happened only once a decade.

46

So it was no surprise that students didn't really pay attention to the team. The mediocrity continued during Jeremy's first two years at Harvard (12-16 his freshman year, 8-22 his sophomore year), but both the Harvard basketball team and Jeremy were a work in progress.

Following Jeremy's freshman year, Harvard assistant coach Lamar Reddicks told the young athlete that he was "the weakest Harvard basketball player that he or the program had ever seen."[1] Jeremy understood the motivation behind the comment, so he started lifting weights for the first time in his life and added muscle to his lanky frame.

The Harvard head coach, Tommy Amaker, who'd been an All-American player at Duke and coached under legendary coach Mike Krzyzewski, liked Jeremy's quickness and his slashing moves to the rim, but the glaring hole in his game was shooting beyond the three-point line.

In college hoops, the three-point line is twenty feet, nine inches (it's between twenty-two feet and twenty-three feet, nine inches in the NBA), so guards are expected to keep defenses off balance by taking the trey — and making it nearly half the time. Jeremy, however, was a 28 percent shooter from behind the arc, and defenses noticed. They'd back off to stop him from driving to the basket and dare him to shoot a three-pointer.

At Coach Amaker's recommendation, Jeremy focused on his outside shooting between his sophomore and junior years. Many mornings he met assistant coach Ken Blakeny at 7 a.m. to work on his shooting mechanics and increase his range.

The dogged approach worked. He soon became a consistent threat to make the three-pointer, and the whole floor opened up to him. "That's why, in Jeremy's junior year, Coach Amaker basically gave him the keys to the bus and said, 'Let's go,'" said Will Wade, one of the Crimson assistant coaches.[2]

With Jeremy behind the wheel, Harvard basketball became relevant again during his junior year, especially after he scored 25 points to help the Crimson beat a Boston College team that was coming off an upset of North Carolina. The team's improvement from 8-22 to 14-14 was significant, and Jeremy's numbers progressed just as dramatically: 17.7 points per game, 4.2 assists, and 40 percent from the three-point line.

Even more noteworthy was that Jeremy earned the distinction as the only NCAA Division I men's basketball player who ranked in the Top 10 in his conference for scoring, rebounding, assists, steals, blocked shots, field goal percentage, free throw percentage, and three-point shooting percentage. He was improving quickly and finding his game, but Jeremy was also determined to be a regular college student.

He lived in the dorms his freshman year and never put on the airs of being someone special because he played on the basketball team. Let's face it: at Harvard, just about *every* student has a special talent in something, and Jeremy was no different. He liked making friends, hanging out, eating too much pizza, and playing Halo, his favorite video game. He was social, but not a partier.

Many young adult Christians, when they go off to

college, fall away from their faith, especially if they attend an elite, secular university like Harvard. Others get swallowed up by the nightly party scene and live selfish lives.

Jeremy, though, didn't step off the "narrow trail" that's talked about in the Bible that leads to a glorious life in Christ. He knew he had to be in God's Word daily, so he read Scripture in the morning and in the evening before the lights went out.

"When I first got to Harvard, I was suddenly around athletes all the time, and I wasn't used to that," Jeremy said. "It's a tough environment, and if you don't have appropriate boundaries, you'll compromise your faith. I struggled spiritually for a while, and I didn't have many Christian friends. It wasn't until I got plugged into a small group my sophomore year that things really started to change. I began to build a Christian community, learn more about Jesus in the Bible, and develop relationships that helped me with accountability."[3]

Going to church every Sunday was difficult due to road trips, but Jeremy attended a local church at Harvard Square, where his cousin was a pastor, as often as he could. The biggest boost in his spiritual growth came when he joined the Harvard-Radcliffe Asian-American Christian Fellowship (HRAACF), because he made friends that he could talk to about Christianity. Jeremy became a co-leader his junior and senior years, and although his involvement with the group was limited by the demands of class work and playing basketball, he met regularly with Adrian Tam, an HRAACF campus staffer.

Adrian became a spiritual mentor to Jeremy, as they

studied the Bible together and read books like *Too Busy Not to Pray*. "He loved his roommates, spending lots of intense one-on-one time with them, leading investigative Bible studies with them, and just plain hanging out with them," Adrian said.

What Adrian remembers most about Jeremy, from their very first meeting, was his humility. "Even though he was more accomplished, smarter, and just plain bigger than I was, he always treated me with respect and honor," Adrian said. "He was real with me, earnestly desiring to follow God in all things. He had a quiet ambition—not only to be the best basketball player he could be, but also to be the best Christ-follower he could be."

One of the best things about being involved with Asian-American Christian Fellowship was seeing fellow students come to Christ and make lifestyle changes.

"When that happens, you definitely see God behind it," Jeremy said. "I'm really thankful God is changing somebody, or sometimes he's changing *me*. To see that transformation brings me a lot of satisfaction and fulfillment. I definitely want to do something in ministry down the road, maybe as a pastor if that's where God leads me."[4]

Following his freshman year in the dorms, Jeremy spent his last three years living at Leverett House, a student housing complex that overlooked the Charles River. He formed a tight-knit group of friends who lived together in an eight-man suite with a common area for studying and socializing. When Leverett House formed a flag football team, Jeremy became the star wide receiver. During the 2009 Harvard intramural flag football championship against archrival Winthrop House, Jeremy proved himself to be quite a pass-catching machine in a 35–20 victory, leaping high for touchdown passes and interceptions.

Although Jeremy showed no fear on the football field, he wasn't so brave when it came time for his annual flu shot. Alek Blankenau, a Leverett House resident and Harvard teammate, recalled a time when the basketball players were directed to get flu vaccinations at the start of the season—a sensible directive given how a flu bug can sweep through a campus. Jeremy was having none of it, though, because of a deep-seated fear of needles.

As the players queued up, Jeremy started to freak out. An agitated Jeremy whispered to Alek that he couldn't do this and wanted to step out of line. "I said, 'Are you serious? We're grown men. You need to get it together,' " Alek recalled. "That was definitely the most flustered I'd ever seen him."

He certainly never looked flustered on the basketball court, where the first green sprouts of Linsanity pushed through the soil during Jeremy's final season at Harvard. The Harvard team rode his back to an unprecedented 21-8 record. As the Crimson kept winning games—and beating conference rivals like Yale, Brown, and Dartmouth—the 2,195-seat bandbox known as Lavietes Pavilion filled up with Harvard students wearing T-shirts that read "Welcome to the Jeremy Lin Show."

Suddenly, showing up at college basketball's second-oldest arena (which opened in 1926) and cheering for Jeremy and *their* team was relevant again at an Ivy

League college normally starved of school spirit. Cheng Ho, the senior running back on the football team, saw a kindred soul in another Asian-American athlete on campus and sprang into action. He started a Facebook campaign called "People of the Crimson" to get people to come to Harvard basketball home games. (Interestingly, Facebook started in Mark Zuckerberg's Harvard dorm room six years earlier.)

Instead of a sparsely populated student section, Lavietes Pavilion was energized by a full house of spirited undergrads, curious alums, and even kids from the poor neighborhoods in nearby East Cambridge—with many of them wearing either "white out" or "black out" T-shirts as directed by the latest Facebook post from Chairman Ho.

Jeremy was a hit with the home crowd; however, the reception was far chillier—even cruel—on the road.

Origin of a Peachy Sport

On a wintry December morning in 1891, Dr. James Naismith nailed wooden peach baskets to the lower rail of the gymnasium balcony, which happened to be ten feet off the ground. He told his class they were going to play a new game and posted thirteen rules on the bulletin board. "Basket Ball" was played with nine players on each team and didn't allow dribbling. The objective: heave a lumpy soccer ball into your basket. The game stopped after every score, because somebody had to climb a ladder to retrieve the ball. Obviously, some things have changed about the sport, but it's a good thing the lower balcony at the Springfield gym wasn't *twelve* feet or we wouldn't have the NBA Slam Dunk Contest every year.

Chapter 8

What's in a Name?

College basketball crowds can be brutal. Duke University's basketball fans, known as the Cameron Crazies because the Blue Devils play in Cameron Indoor Stadium, have the reputation for being among the most spirited in the country. Have you ever heard a crowd chant "air ball" after a player totally misses the basket with a shot? That started at Duke.

But sometimes the Crazies go a bit too ... crazy. They've been known to throw Twinkies at overweight players on opposing teams or shout "We're smart! You're dumb!" during games against rival North Carolina.

So it should come as no surprise that the sight of an Asian-American basketball player—whose all-over-the-floor style was beating their team—would prompt a few immature members of student sections to taunt Jeremy.

During Harvard away games, some fans yelled really

stupid (and racist) stuff, like "Hey, sweet and sour pork" or "wonton soup" from the stands. "Go back to China" and "The orchestra is on the other side of campus" were other dim-witted taunts. One time at Georgetown, Jeremy heard terribly unkind remarks aimed in his direction, including the racial slur "slant eyes."

It wasn't the first time Jeremy had heard these words. Even in high school, mean-spirited comments were shouted his way.

At first, Jeremy admitted that the names would bother him and affect his play. But then he remembered passages in the Bible that said to "turn the other cheek" and just forgive. After all, Jesus forgave his tormentors who shouted cruel words at him as he hung on the cross. Jeremy followed his Savior's example and determined to play harder and let his game speak for itself. In the process, he helped make Harvard relevant in college basketball.

During his senior year, Jeremy also tried to let his faith show more on the court.

"I've learned how to be open and bold about my faith, but in terms of my influence," Jeremy said. "I just try to lead in a godly way. What that means for me is to serve, whether it's doing the dirty work, like cleaning up sweat on the floor or carrying equipment bags. In basketball these days, the rookies and freshmen are supposed to do the grunt work and seniors relax and hang out. When you reverse that ... it shows you're trying to serve them, and that's a good way to lead."[1]

As a senior, Jeremy was again among the top Ivy League players in ten offensive categories. His scoring

Nick Wass/AP Images

Jeremy put the Harvard basketball program on the map, leading the team to a 21-8 record his senior year.

average was 16.4 points per game, which is remarkable because he only took an average of 9.9 shots per game, a vivid example of his unselfish play. For the third year in a row, he won Raymond P. Lavietes '36 MVP award, voted on by teammates. He also earned a spot in the record books at Harvard: first all-time in games played (115), fifth in points (1,483), fifth in assists (406), and second in steals (225).

Jeremy's inspired play even caught the eye of the media, especially during a two-week stretch early in the season.

At the end of November, Jeremy scored his team's last 11 points in a 78–70 victory over cross-town rival Boston University. Then a week later, his stock rose higher when Harvard traveled to play then number 12-ranked University of Connecticut, a traditional college basketball powerhouse. He dissected and bisected UConn for 30 points and nine rebounds and threw a scare into one of the top teams in the country. Harvard lost 79–73, but Jeremy earned a new set of admirers.

Reporters from up and down the East Coast flocked to learn more about the Jeremy Lin Show. They wanted to measure the player who'd turned around a perennially weak Ivy League program.

Pretty soon Jeremy was being called by other, much kinder, names. Here are some of the more memorable quotes:

- "Jeremy Lin is probably one of the best players in the country you don't know about" (ESPN's Rece Davis).

- "He is a joy to watch. He's smooth, smart, unself-ish, and sees the floor like no one else on it sees" (*Boston Herald* columnist Len Megliola).

- "Keep an eye on Harvard's Jeremy Lin. The fact that he's an Asian-American guard playing at Harvard has probably kept him off the NBA radar too long. But as scouts are hunting everywhere for point guards, more and more are coming back and acknowledging that Lin is a legit prospect" (ESPN NBA draft analyst Chad Ford).[2]

Sports Illustrated did their first major feature on Jeremy in February 2010, entitled "Harvard School of Basketball." Writer Pablo S. Torre zipped off this description:

It's a mid-January afternoon, and the senior econ major driving the unlikeliest revival in college basketball sits in his fourth-floor dorm room overlooking a frozen Charles River. He's surrounded by photos of family and friends back in Palo Alto, Calif., a poster of Warriors-era Chris Webber, and an Xbox in disrepair. Nothing suggests Lin's status as the first finalist in more than a decade for the Wooden award and first for the Cousy award (nation's top point guard) to come from the scholarship-devoid Ivies.

"I never could have predicted any of this," says Lin. "To have people talk about you like that? I'm not really used to it."[3]

Only fifteen finalists are named for the John Wooden Award, the nation's most coveted college basketball honor. Jeremy knew he had a better chance at winning the Bob Cousy Award as the nation's top point guard (named after Hall of Famer and former Boston Celtics guard Bob Cousy), but Maryland guard Greivis Vasquez, who grew up playing street basketball in the barrios of Caracas, Venezuela, received the honor.

When Jeremy's playing career at Harvard ended, he graduated on time with a degree in economics (he minored in sociology) and a 3.1 grade-point average. He had high hopes that an NBA team would draft him and give him a shot at making the roster. But there was a prevailing headwind fighting against him.

First, he didn't play in a major college conference against the biggest, tallest, and best college players in the land.

And his ethnicity?

Let's not go there, but the 800-pound gorilla in the draft room was that no Taiwanese-American player had ever worn an NBA uniform. If Jeremy was going to do it, he would have to be the first.

Reaching the highest level of professional basketball is extremely difficult. Around 3,600 men have played in the NBA since its inception in 1949, but how many have tried to get there—or imagined doing so? The answer has to be in the tens of millions, if you count every boy who has pretended to be Michael or Magic or Dwyane or Jerry in the driveway, dribbling toward the basket to score the winning shot in Game 7 of the NBA Finals.

Jeremy was one of those kids who played hoops for hours in the driveway. When he was in middle school, he and his brothers would sometimes stop playing and peer through the window when Dad had an NBA game on TV. Jeremy would see Michael Jordan make one of his patented fadeaway jumpers, and then he'd return to the driveway and imitate the move, over and over.

Jeremy had been practicing and playing basketball since he was five years old. Yet despite all the hard work he put in to develop his God-given talent, the way Jeremy made it to the NBA happened in God's economy.

In other words, it was a miracle.

California Road Trip

During Jeremy's senior year, the basketball program at Santa Clara University, located fifteen miles from Jeremy's hometown of Palo Alto, invited Harvard to the West Coast for a "homecoming" game.

News of the match up created a buzz in the San Francisco Bay Area.

"If you want to see an arena filled with thousands of Asian-Americans rooting for the best Asian-American basketball player ever, you should come to this historic game," wrote a blogger on the Golden State of Mind website, urging everyone to wear black in support of Harvard's road uniforms.[4]

And thousands of Jeremy Lin fans wearing black T-shirts did come on January 4, 2010, as they packed the 4,700-seat Leavey Center to capacity. The pressure of playing before parents and family, his old buddies from high school and youth basketball days, and his new fans took its toll. Jeremy suffered through a case of butterflies and scored only six points. He ran the offense well, though, in helping Harvard defeat Santa Clara 74–66.

Chapter 9

Undrafted and Unwanted

Ed Welland is a draft geek, the type of guy who sifts through statistics like gold panners looking for nuggets of key information.

He studied the crop of point guards on the draft board and said the pickings for playmakers were going to be thin in 2010. "That doesn't mean there won't be a player or two who surprise the experts though," Welland wrote. "The best candidate to pull off such a surprise might be Harvard's Jeremy Lin. The reason is two numbers Lin posted, 2-point PG pct and RSB40. Lin was at .598 and 9.7. This is impressive on both counts. These numbers show NBA athleticism better than any other, because a high score in both shows dominance at the college level on both ends of the court."[1]

It would take a Harvard math major to explain the details behind APBRmetrics (which stands for Association for Professional Basketball Research), but basically Welland was saying that Jeremy's high field goal percent inside the 3-point line—making six out of ten shots or .598 percent—along with his ability to rebound, steal, and block—that's the RSB40 statistic—made him a 24-karat gold prospect.

But what did Ed Welland know? He drove a FedEx delivery truck in a small eastern Oregon town and published his assessments on the sports blog *hoopsanalyst.com*. When he chose Jeremy as his top point guard prospect, he had never seen him play since Harvard games weren't easily viewable in a lonely outpost such as Bend, Oregon. Welland made the call solely on the statistics printed on a spreadsheet.

NBA scouts relied more on visual assessments, which are more subjective. In the run-up to the 2010 NBA draft, Jeremy got some looks. He was invited to work-out with eight teams, including his hometown Golden State Warriors. Yet when the big day came, Jeremy was passed over in the two-round draft that selected only sixty players. Playing at an Ivy League school probably had a lot to do with that. The last Harvard player to wear an NBA jersey was Ed Smith, who played just eleven games in his one-season career in 1953–54. The conventional wisdom among pro scouts was that Harvard players never panned out in the NBA.

Jeremy did catch a break when Dallas general manager Donnie Nelson invited him to play on the Mavericks' Summer League team after the draft noise settled down. NBA Summer League games are played at frenetic pace, and they can be a bit sloppy. But for rookies and players looking for a team, Summer League provides a fleeting chance—perhaps a *last* chance—to pit their skills against NBA-level competition and make an impression. This particular eight-day summertime season took place in Las Vegas in July, 2010.

Jeremy wasn't a starter for the Mavericks' Summer League team, not by a long shot. He sat behind an electrifying point guard named Rodrigue Beaubois, whom Dallas coaches were appraising for a roster spot. In the first four games, Jeremy was a substitute who averaged 17 minutes and eight points a game.

Then some interesting events happened that changed the arc of Jeremy's basketball life, things that Jeremy believes were orchestrated by the hand of God:

1. Jeremy's team played the Washington Wizards' Summer League team, which featured John Wall, the 2010 number 1 overall draft pick. Wall would be named the Summer League MVP that season.

2. This was the last contest of the five-game Summer League season. A large number of scouts and NBA team officials were on hand.

3. Rodrigue Beaubois twisted an ankle and had a poor outing in the first half. Jeremy took his place.

4. By all accounts, Jeremy outplayed, outhustled, outdrove, and outshined Wall in the second half while leading his team to a big comeback—drawing oohs and ahs from the crowd with several

Jeremy's big break came during the final game of the July 2010 NBA Summer League, when he outplayed, outhustled, and outshone his opponents, impressing NBA scouts.

fearless drives to the rim. During the fourth quarter, Jeremy's tenacious defense on Wall forced a jump ball. He then came out of nowhere to make a sensational steal. Later, Jeremy tore a rebound out of the hands of a seven-foot center. For the game, he hit six of twelve shots, including his only 3-point try of the night.

After that single half of brilliant play, several NBA teams looked at Jeremy in a new light. The Mavericks, the Los Angeles Lakers, and the Golden State Warriors all thought that with the right seasoning, he could develop into an NBA player. Their thinking was that Jeremy could play a season in the NBA's Development League—known as D-League—and see where that took him.

And then Joe Lacob entered the picture.

During the summer of 2010, Lacob was in the midst of purchasing the Golden State Warriors with Peter Guber, the former chairman of Sony Pictures. Together, they put a $450 million tender to buy the team.

So how did this affect Jeremy?

Well, it turns out that Lacob—living in the Bay Area—had coached his son's youth basketball team, which played against Jeremy when he was younger.

This fascinating exchange between Lacob and *San Jose Mercury News* columnist Tim Kawakami explains things:

Let's just confirm that you made the call to sign Jeremy Lin.

Lacob: It was my call.

Why Lin?

Lacob: Well, that's a special situation.

Your son played with Lin? Against Lin?

Lacob: There were probably three guys that were pretty much the best point guards in high school in this area at that time, and Jeremy Lin was probably the best of them. And my son, Kirk, was right there with him. I've watched them play against each other, and I've coached against him since he was this high.

So I know him from [the time he was] a little kid. Also at Palo Alto I watched him win the state championship over a superior team, and he dominated Mater Dei. And he has heart, he has a lot of talent, he's athletic, which a lot of people don't understand. He's pretty long.

He has a game that translates to the NBA. He can drive, he's a slasher. He needs to shoot better, obviously. He needs to be a better outside shooter.

It's funny, people don't know his game. They say, oh, he's a shooter but he doesn't have these other skills. No, that's not true, it's the opposite....

If you watched his tape, if you watched him in the John Wall thing in Vegas, he played John Wall even up. This is not a guy that shouldn't have been drafted. This is a guy that should've been drafted.

Doesn't that put some pressure on a coach to play him?

Jeremy was all smiles with his parents, Shirley and Gie-Ming, when he signed a two-year contract in the summer of 2010 to play for his hometown team, the Golden State Warriors.

Lacob: No, he's got to prove it on the court.

You'll be watching.

Lacob: That's not for me to determine. He has to prove it, coaches have to coach him, and we'll see. Jeremy should've obviously gotten recruited to Stanford. Made a huge error. And by the way, there were a lot of us who were Stanford boosters who were trying to get them to recruit Jeremy. They did not. Well, guess what, that was really stupid. I'm a big Stanford fan, but that was really stupid. The kid was right across the street. You can't recognize that, you've got a problem.[2]

And that's how Jeremy Lin got his chance to play in the NBA. Two weeks after Summer League, he signed a two-year contract with the Warriors. News of his signing sent a shockwave of excitement through the San Francisco Bay Area—especially the Asian-American community. Then, through tenacity and grit in training camp, he won a spot on the Warriors' roster.

Undrafted, fighting for recognition, and given the slimmest of opportunities, Jeremy had somehow beaten incredible odds to put on an NBA jersey.

Even better, his hometown team wanted him—and so did the hometown fans.

Getting a Draft

At just two rounds, the NBA draft is the shortest of all major professional sports. Here's how other drafts stack up:

Major League Baseball

The MLB has the longest amateur draft. A baseball draft can last fifty rounds and have more than 1,500 players selected. Baseball players started being picked this way in 1965.

National Football League

The first NFL draft occurred on February 8, 1936. Today, the NFL's seven-round draft (which chooses around 250 players) is almost a spectator sport in itself. The draft is televised and sports writers make a living guessing which college players will go to which team.

National Hockey League

The NHL draft also goes seven rounds. Only professional hockey and baseball teams can draft high-school aged athletes. Around 215 players are chosen in the NHL draft, which officially began in 1963.

Chapter 10

Rookie Blues

After signing with the Warriors, Jeremy got his own place in Hayward, California, located roughly midway between his parents' home in Palo Alto and the Oracle Arena in Oakland, where the Warriors play.

When training camp started, Jeremy discovered he wasn't as ready for the NBA as he thought. His teammates outperformed him in practice drills, which only heightened his anxiety and sagged his confidence. Even his coaches' encouragement couldn't lift his spirits. "I was humbled very quickly," he said, describing that rude awakening as a roller-coaster ride between euphoria and despair.[1] He made the team, but just barely. Jeremy chose to wear number 7—the biblical number that expresses completeness or perfection—on his jersey.

He sat on the bench for a season-opening win against the Houston Rockets but made his NBA debut two nights later in Golden State's second game of the 2010–11 season. On "Asian Heritage Night," a packed house of 17,408 fans exploded with cheers when Jeremy came into the game with two and a half minutes to go— and the Warriors comfortably ahead. He had the honor of dribbling out the final seconds of a hometown win over the Los Angeles Clippers.

Jeremy Lin had made history, becoming the first Chinese/Taiwanese-American basketball player to step onto a 94-by-50-foot NBA hardwood court. The only other full-blooded American-born Asian to play professional basketball in the United States was five-foot, seven-inch Wataru "Kilo Wat" Misaka. He played in only *three* games for the New York Knickerbockers back in 1947—in the old Basketball Association of America (BAA), which would become the NBA two years later. Born to Japanese immigrants, Misaka deserves honorable mention for being a pioneer at a time when Allied forces had just defeated Japan in World War II and memories of Japanese Army atrocities were still fresh in the public's memory.

More importantly, "Kilo Wat," who entered the league during the same year Jackie Robinson broke the color barrier in Major League Baseball, was the first non-Caucasian to play professional basketball—a noteworthy achievement since it would be another three years before the NBA admitted its first black player in 1950.

Through the 2011–12 season, there have been four other American players—Raymond Townsend, Corey Gaines, Rex Walters, and Robert Swift—who played in the NBA

Jeff Chiu/AP Images

In Golden State's second home game of the 2010–2011 season on "Asian Heritage Night," 17,408 fans exploded with cheers when Jeremy played his first minutes in the NBA.

and came from a mixed heritage, such as an American father married to a Japanese or Filipino mother.

During those early games with the Warriors, Jeremy hustled and played hard, but it was evident that he was worried about making mistakes, which often causes a player to be less aggressive in a hardnosed professional game where boldness and determination separate those who make it from those who are looking for a new job.

Jeremy's newfound notoriety added to the pressure. An immediate blast of attention came from media heavyweights — *NBC Nightly News*, *The New York Times*, and *Time* magazine, to name a few — who wrote glowing features about the first Asian-American to play in the NBA. Jeremy thought he was grounded enough to withstand the media examination as well as thousands of requests to "friend" him on Facebook, but he soon learned otherwise. Even though the local fans loved cheering for their native son, the focused attention created an intense spotlight that followed him everywhere. It started showing on the court. Soon it was apparent that he was a work in progress as a basketball player.

In late December, 2010, the Warriors reassigned Jeremy — who had averaged 17 minutes a game — to their D-League affiliate, the Reno Bighorns.

Near despair, Jeremy wrote in his personal journal that he felt like a failure after putting so much pressure on himself to make the NBA. During a conference hosted by River of Life Christian Church in Santa Clara after the season was over, Jeremy said he wrote this entry into his personal journal on December 29, 2010:

Jeff Chiu/AP Images

Jeremy would go on to warm the bench and play in only 29 games for the Warriors, and was sent three times to the Reno Bighorns, the Warriors' D-League affiliate, to work on his game and get some playing time.

This is probably the closest to depression I've been. I lack confidence on the court. I'm not having fun playing basketball anymore. I hate being in the D-League, and I want to rejoin the Warriors. I feel embarrassed and like a failure.[2]

If you think about it, Jeremy had never "failed" at anything before. He'd been a straight-A student, posted high SAT scores, graduated from Harvard, and turned himself into one of the best college basketball players in the country. But the NBA was a tough challenge, which only stands to reason since many experts believe it contains the world's best athletes.

In short, basketball players must possess sprinter speed, extraordinary height, quick lateral motion, great coordination, and Superman-like jumping ability.

> **NBA players . . .**
> - are taller and stronger than 99.999999 percent of the world's population
> - can run like gazelles while maintaining a dribble
> - can stop on a dime and successfully shoot a ball through a rim that has a seventeen-inch diameter (about an inch less than twice the diameter of the basketball)
> - show impressive athleticism and "hang time" when driving toward the rim

Jeremy had come so far — like pounding a pivot board with a mallet and watching the metal striker rise within inches of hitting a bell. But instead of going home with a prize, Jeremy was demoted to the D-League.

"It was a shock [going to Reno] because I did not realize how different the two leagues were," he said. "It was also humbling because the locker rooms, facilities, attendance at games, the travel — it was all very different."

On New Year's Day 2011, he wrote in his journal, "I wish I had never signed with the Warriors."

Jeremy did some soul-searching and came to this conclusion: "None of the paychecks, the car, the fame, none of the NBA lifestyle, none of that stuff, my dream job, my dream life, none of that meant anything to me anymore," Jeremy said. "My happiness was dependent on how well I played."[3]

Stripped of everything else, Jeremy realized his happiness was derived from seeing shots swish through the net, receiving atta-boys from coaches, and hearing explosive cheers from the fans. Deep down he knew those things were temporal. Basketball had become an idol in his life. Jeremy was wise enough to figure out that if he was dependent on a game as the source of his happiness, then he was destined to become one unhappy young man. He recommitted himself to putting God first and trusting him for the future. That decision gave Jeremy a whole new perspective. The lesson learned was that success is fleeting, but humility is eternal.

"I had a lot of long nights and struggles, learning how to submit my will to God and trust him through different situations that I thought were maybe unfair at times," Jeremy said.

Even though he wished his basketball career was going a different way, Jeremy leaned more on God, and spent a lot of time reading the Bible and praying.

"I did more praying than I had ever done," Jeremy said. "And I learned a ton."

Being sent down to Reno was a trial. In the Bible,

James 1:2 promised believers of Jesus Christ that they would face adversities of many kinds. But it wasn't the end of the world—or the end of his NBA aspirations. Knowing that allowed Jeremy to have a total attitude adjustment: If going down to D-League was what the Warriors wanted him to do, then that's what he'd do. He'd listen to his coaches, work on his weaknesses, and play hard.

He'd also continue to live out his faith and serve others. When the team traveled by airplane to places like Erie, New York, Canton, Ohio, or the border town of Hidalgo, Texas, Jeremy was entitled to roomier first-class seating since he was on assignment from the Warriors. The regular roster players on the Bighorns had to sit in the cramped economy class. Wedging their six-foot, nine-inch bodies into tiny airplane seats was a gymnastic trick worthy of a Cirque du Soleil production.

Jeremy always gave up his first-class ticket to a taller teammate and sat in the back of the plane. "That really spoke volumes about what type of guy he is," said Eric Musselman, his coach on the Reno Bighorns. "Our players loved playing with him."[4]

Jeremy played well in Reno, averaging 18 points, 5.6 rebounds, and 4.3 assists a game. He logged a lot of minutes on the court and gained some much-needed experience playing in the pros.

He wasn't confident yet, but he was a lot more comfortable, a lot more at ease when he was in the game, and that showed in his improved play ... which eventually earned him another shot with the Warriors.

Jersey Night Done Right

Following the rise of Linsanity, the Reno Bighorns' front office knew a good promotion when they saw one. For their March 17, 2012, game, they had "Jeremy Lin Giveaway Night" and handed out 1,500 limited edition jerseys — even though the former star was no longer playing for the Golden State Warriors' organization. The jerseys went like proverbial hotcakes, but can only be found on eBay now.

Chapter 11

The Tempting Life of the NBA

Playing nearly as many games for the Reno Bighorns (twenty) as he did with the Golden State Warriors (twenty-nine), Jeremy discovered that the NBA was not an easy gig. The long season had players bouncing from city to city like a ball in a pinball machine. The physical strain of performing on back-to-back nights in different cities fatigued the legs. Even the best-conditioned athletes found they had to pace themselves during the season—even during games—so they had something in reserve for a fourth-quarter rally.

Besides the physical demands, Christian hoopsters like Jeremy have it even tougher because of temptations that bombard them daily. They are presented with numerous opportunities to compromise their values and follow worldly desires. Without overstating it, NBA players face challenges and temptations that are nearly impossible to comprehend. They have money, lots of free time on their hands, and flocks of women trying to catch their eye in hotel lobbies, restaurants, and bars. Often dressed provocatively, these women hope to develop a relationship with a millionaire athlete.

"Most people forget that we're talking about kids in their early twenties," said Jeff Ryan, the chaplain for the Orlando Magic. "If you can remember your early twenties, and I can remember mine, you don't always make the right choices. I was fortunate that I didn't have the temptations that these guys have. Remember, they are targeted. Some handle it well, and some don't. Unfortunately, there are plenty of guys who get caught up in the women thing and get their heads turned. They come into the league with the best of intentions, wanting to be faithful, wanting to be strong, but they give in to temptation."

Before Jeremy set foot in the NBA, his mom and dad warned him about the temptations he'd encounter.

"They said, 'Be smart. There are going to be girls throwing themselves at you, so be smart,'" Jeremy said. "They also reminded me to make sure that I took care of my relationship with God first."

Because Jeremy had his eyes wide open, his faith as a priority, and good Christian teammates, he said after his rookie season: "I don't want to say it was easy, but it wasn't as bad as I thought it would be. It helped that I had a couple of teammates who were strong Christians—Stephen Curry and Reggie Williams. We would go to chapel together before the games, and we would occasionally have Christian conversations, so that was definitely helpful. I had a lot of accountability in terms of a small group. And I was at home playing for the Warriors, so I went to my home church whenever I could."

Having his family nearby made the transition into the pros a lot easier, but his busy schedule made getting to church difficult. Often he listened to sermons on his computer on Sunday. His dad also burned a bunch of sermons for him onto CDs, so he carried them around in a case and listened whenever he got the chance.

On road trips — that can last from five to seven days — Jeremy didn't stray too far from the hotel.

"I didn't go out very much," Jeremy explained about his strategy to avoid temptations. "There were guys on my team that I hung out with, and we had a different lifestyle, so it wasn't a huge issue. It's definitely out there if you want it, but I chose to take it out of play. Once you take a stand for something at the beginning, everybody respects that and they don't bother you about it."

Instead of experiencing the nightlife in the different cities he traveled to, Jeremy spent his nights digging into God's Word and doing devotions in his hotel room.

"I had more time to spend with God than I have ever had," Jeremy said. "That was one of the parts that made it easier versus in college, where you wake up, go to class, practice, then do your homework, and go to sleep."

After bouncing back and forth between Reno and Golden State, Jeremy finished the last two weeks of the season with the parent club and ended on a high note.

In the Warriors' final game in mid-April, he scored 12 points and played 24 minutes in a win over the Portland Trailblazers. That was much better than the typical DNP (Did Not Play) that often appeared next to Jeremy's name in the box score. For the season, he averaged 9.8 minutes and scored 2.6 points per game for a struggling Golden State team that finished 36–46 and failed to make the playoffs.

Jeremy's rookie season didn't go like he'd hoped, but he stayed positive about the future. "I just know that this is where God wants me right now," he said. "This past year I have gone through a lot of different struggles and learned to draw me closer to God, humble myself, and be more dependent on him."

He had signed a two-year contract with Golden State, so he expected the team would continue to bring him along, give him more playing time, and help him become the best player he could be.

Funny how things worked out.

Lessons from a Legend

Tennis star Michael Chang may be the greatest — and most famous — Asian-American athlete ever. In 1989, he became the youngest male to win a Grand Slam tournament when he captured the French Open at the age of seventeen. During his fourteen-year Hall of Fame career, Michael rose to number 2 in the tennis world.

Before Jeremy's rookie season with the Golden State Warriors, he talked with Michael about being a Christian in professional sports.

"I picked up some good ideas," Jeremy said, "like having a consistent devotional time and a prayer team behind you. So I formed a little team that I sent e-mails to every once in a while with prayer requests and praise reports."

The fact that Jeremy reached out to Michael for advice on athletic *and* spiritual matters reveals a lot about his character. Michael's answers — and the fact that he continues to send Jeremy encouraging text messages — reveal a lot about his.

"I think it's great that Jeremy is so outspoken about his faith," Michael said. "People are a little less likely to ask you to do something or be a part of something, knowing that your faith takes first precedence in your life. I think Jeremy has a good head on his shoulders.... He is very humble, gives a lot of credit to the Knicks' staff, and is very complimentary toward his fellow players. Hopefully, he'll be a great influence on them, not only on the basketball court but off it as well."

Chapter 12

Locked Out, But Locked In

With NBA owners and the Players Association unable to agree on a new contract, the 2011 NBA lockout began on July 1. As the fourth lockout in league history, it nearly forced the entire 2011–12 season to be canceled. As it was, the 161-day work stoppage ended on December 8, 2011. The lockout delayed the start of the regular season from November 1 to Christmas Day, and reduced the regular season from eighty-two to sixty-six games.

During the lockout, Jeremy could not step inside the Warriors' gleaming training facility in downtown Oakland. Nor was he allowed any contact with the coaches, trainers, or staff. Jeremy had to motivate himself to stay in shape. That wasn't a problem, because he was locked in on improving his physical assets and his game. He worked harder than ever to be ready when the NBA started up again.

His schedule included:

- 10–11 a.m.: agility training
- 11–noon: weight training
- 1–2 p.m.: shooting work with a private coach
- 2–4 p.m.: individual work[1]

He posted YouTube videos of his maniacal workouts on the court and in the weight room with trainer Phil Wagner. And his results were impressive: he tripled the number of pull-ups he could do (from twelve to thirty), doubled the weight he could squat (from 110 pounds to 231 pounds), added twelve pounds of muscle to his 200-pound frame, and boosted his vertical leap by three and a half inches.

He also worked on a hitch in his shooting mechanics that dated back to eighth grade. Doc Scheppler, the girls' basketball coach at Pinewood High School in Los Altos Hills, California, noticed that he brought the ball too far behind his head, which hurt his rhythm on the release. Scheppler taught him how to "load" his shot earlier and release the ball in rhythm at the apex of his jump. They practiced ninety minutes a day, three to four times a week, taking 500 to 600 shots each session.

"That's the lesson here," Scheppler said. "If you don't like the way things are going for you in a sport, don't cry about it. Don't whine to the coach. Do something about it."[2] Through this process, Jeremy reengineered himself, shot by shot and pound by pound.

Meanwhile, he kept an eye on the latest news of contract negotiations between the NBA owners and the player's union. As each "deadline" passed without an agreement, both sides inched closer to the unthinkable—losing the entire season.

At the eleventh hour, an agreement was reached on November 25, 2011. NBA commissioner David Stern announced that the first practice would be Friday, December 9, with the official season beginning on Christmas Day.

Jeremy arrived at the Oakland facility for the first day of practice and suited up. He had just met his new coach, Mark Jackson, who had never seen him play. Undoubtedly, Jeremy felt mounting pressure to prove himself all over again.

He was loosening up when he found out that general manager Larry Riley wanted to see him. The Warriors hadn't even started their layup drills.

If you've seen the movie *Moneyball*, you know it's never good news when the GM asks to see you. This occasion was no exception.

Jeremy, the Warriors organization has decided to put you on waivers. We think you'll clear the waiver wire so that we'll get you back.

No matter how much Riley tried to spin it, the pronouncement stunk. Jeremy was being cut from the team. For all he knew, his short-lived NBA career was over.

This is where the "business" side of professional basketball can destroy a player's dream in a heartbeat. What happened is that the Golden State management made a calculated decision to go after Los Angeles Clipper center DeAndre Jordan, a restricted free agent, to shore up a deficiency in rebounding and inside scoring. To make Jordan an offer he couldn't refuse, the Warriors had to create room under their salary cap. That meant moving around a few pieces: cut Jeremy loose, use their amnesty clause on veteran guard Charlie Bell, and delay the signing of two rookies they liked—Klay Thompson and Jeremy Tyler. Then, under salary cap rules, the team would have enough money to bring in the center they desperately needed.

Once Jordan was signed, sealed, and delivered, the Warriors could bring back Jeremy, if no other team claimed him.

On the same day—December 9—something important to Jeremy's future occurred in New York. The Knicks waived veteran point guard Chauncey Billups and signed center Tyson Chandler, leaving the team out of cap space and without a true point guard.

Three days later, the Houston Rockets claimed Jeremy off of waivers, so he couldn't go back to his childhood team. To add insult to injury, Clippers owner Donald Sterling matched Golden State's overly generous four-year, $43 million offer for DeAndre Jordan, which meant the bruising center would stay in Los Angeles.

Talk about collateral damage. Golden State's gamble had blown up in its face, and Jeremy was starting over with a new team in Houston.

Jeremy arrived in Space City to discover he'd have to wait his turn to make an impression on the coaches. The Rockets were overstocked with point guards, and Jeremy had a hard time getting reps in practice. In two preseason games with the Rockets, he played for a total of sixteen minutes.

"At the time, I was thinking if this doesn't work out, I maybe needed to take a break from basketball," Jeremy said. "I put in four months of training. I felt like I worked harder than anyone else. And now I was fighting for my chance to practice. I was questioning everything."[3]

Then, on Christmas Eve, Jeremy woke up to find a lump of coal in his stocking—he was being waived by Houston. This time GM Daryl Morey was the bearer of bad news, and he didn't salve the wound by saying that he hoped Jeremy would be back. He explained that the Rockets needed cap room to sign center Samuel Dalembert.

Merry Christmas, kid. Best of luck to you.

This could have been the end of the line. Yet Jeremy knew this latest setback was not the time to doubt if God was still in control. It was the time to press ahead, fully committed to the Lord's plan ... whatever it was.

The day after Christmas, Jeremy woke up at his parents' house and did a devotional before heading to the gym to stay in shape. During his shoot-around, each time anxiety about the future crept in, he whispered Romans 8:28 to himself:

And we know that in all things God works for the good of those who love him, who have been called according to his purpose.

Something good was about to happen, he was sure of it. But Jeremy had no idea that more trials were ahead.

Worth His Weight in Golden State

During the 2011–12 season, Golden State Warriors owners Joe Lacob and Peter Guber were looking to bolster the team's value so they could get higher cable TV revenue and a better arena.

Bob Dorfman, a sports business expert at Baker Street Advertising in San Francisco, said the Warriors would be worth $10 million *more* if Jeremy Lin was still on the team. Dorfman pointed to extra tickets, concessions, and merchandise sales driven by Linsanity. But team sponsorships and potential tourism dollars (from Asian fans coming to the Bay area to see him play) also would've helped.

"Lin was beginning to create a buzz, showing flashes of brilliance, and definitely inspiring the large Bay Area Asian markets," Dorfman said. "But with Monta Ellis and Stephen Curry ahead of him, his playing time dwindled and the hoopla quickly faded."[4]

As quickly as Jeremy faded on one coast, he rose to stardom on the other.

Chapter 13

New York State of Mind

The New York Knicks had a guard problem.

When the lockout ended, the club signed thirty-two-year-old Baron Davis to be their point guard, even though he had a back injury that would keep him out through the end of February. Until Davis could join the team, the Knicks would forge ahead with veteran guards Mike Bibby and Toney Douglas at point and Iman Shumpert as a shooting guard. Bill Walker (six feet, six inches) and Landry Fields (six feet, seven inches) could play in the backcourt, although their natural position was at small forward.

Then in the Christmas Day season opener against the Boston Celtics, Iman Shumpert injured his right knee when he tangled with another player going for a rebound. After the game, the team medical staff called the injury a sprained medial collateral ligament and said Shumpert would need two to four weeks to heal.

The Knicks were down to two guards.

John Gabriel, the director of pro and free agent scouting for the Knicks, said every team looking for a point guard has a certain player in mind. "You want somebody who has good size. He can make the open shot and is getting better on defense. Leadership was looking for someone who would be good at running [coach Mike D'Antoni's] system. That includes making shots, running the floor, being able to push the ball during transition, as well as defend. Those were desired key attributes."

Paging Magic Johnson.

Unfortunately Magic wasn't available, and neither was John Stockton or Walt "Clyde" Frazier. Knicks general manager Glen Grunwald and his assistant GM Allan Houston searched the waiver wire for who was available—and Jeremy Lin's name popped up.

Actually, Jeremy wasn't an unknown commodity to the Knicks' front office staff. He'd been on the Knicks' radar after he made some noise at Harvard.

"We liked him," Grunwald said. "We worked him out in the draft. We had discussions with Golden State when he was there. It was just an opportunity to acquire him when we needed someone who had his skill set."[1]

The Knicks' brain trust saw in the video breakdown more athleticism than they anticipated. Jeremy was a good decision maker. He was worth the risk.

On December 27, the team claimed Jeremy off of waivers to fill a void at backup point guard, prompting Knicks head coach Mike D'Antoni to say, "Yeah, we picked up Jeremy Lin off of waivers [as] a backup point [guard] in case. We've always liked him as a player, so we'll see where we go with it."[2]

Reaction among the New York media was more muted. "The Knicks' offense didn't get a huge boost Tuesday, but their collective GPA sure did," mused *New York Daily News* writer Sean Brennan, referring to the new Ivy Leaguer in their midst.[3]

Jeremy didn't see it that way. He hit his Twitter account and sent out this message: "Thankful to God for the opportunity to be a New York Knick!! Time to find my winter coats from college lol!"

He was back in the NBA, but his contract wasn't guaranteed until February 10. Up until that date, he could be cut any time, so there was no reason to move into a Fifth Avenue penthouse.

Fortunately, at this time Jeremy's big brother, Josh, lived in Manhattan, attending New York University as a dental student. Josh had married, and he and his wife, Patricia, had set up housekeeping in a one-bedroom apartment in the Lower East Side. So if Jeremy didn't mind sleeping on the couch, he had a place to stay.

In his early days as a Knick, Jeremy had to do some fast-talking each time he tried to pass through the player's entrance before home games. "Everytime i try to get into Madison Square Garden, the security guards ask me if im a trainer LOL," he tweeted.[4]

Danny Moloshok/Reuters/Landov

Jeremy was waived by the Golden State Warriors and the Houston Rockets before joining the New York Knicks. Here he warms up with teammate Carmelo Anthony in late December, 2011, when Linsanity was more than a month away.

In spite of D'Antoni's initial positive comments about acquiring Jeremy, he stayed parked at the end of the bench like a wheel clamp was strapped to his Nikes. D'Antoni rarely called his number, which was number 17. His favorite, number 7, wasn't available because Carmelo Anthony already wore it.

During a press conference at the NBA All-Star weekend, Jeremy explained how he came to wear 17. The 1 represented himself and the number 7 represented God. "When I went to D-League, I had 17, and so everywhere

I would go, [God] would be right there next to me. And so that's why I stuck with 17."[5]

From December 28 to January 16, Jeremy played sixteen minutes in twelve games, scoring a total of nine points. Since the Knicks were losing more than they won, there was no way Jeremy could get into the offensive flow at the end of the game after the outcome had already been decided and the play tended to be more chaotic. Plus, he couldn't learn D'Antoni's system because there were very few practice days in the lockout-shortened season.

On January 17, Jeremy was demoted to the Erie BayHawks, the Knicks' D-League team.

Not again!

"I had no opportunity to prove myself," he said. "There was definitely a little bit of 'What's going on?' in my prayers. My flesh was constantly pulling at me. Whine. Complain. Whine. Complain. But the other side of me was thinking, *My God is all powerful ... why do I even doubt God?* At the same time, it's a growing process."[6]

At least he'd get to play ball again. In his BayHawks debut against the Maine Red Claws on January 20, Jeremy laid down a triple double: 28 points, 12 assists, and 11 rebounds. He played forty-five of the forty-eight minutes and repeatedly beat defenders with an extremely quick first step.

The Knicks' scouts were impressed, as they should have been. New York recalled Jeremy. But throughout the rest of January and early February, losses piled up

Bill Kostroun/AP Images

The Knicks had lost two of their last thirteen games when star player Carmelo Anthony suggested to head coach Mike D'Antoni that he put Jeremy into the game against the New Jersey Nets on February 4, 2012. Jeremy led the Knicks to victory, scoring 25 points off the bench, and was named a starter, setting off Linsanity.

like snowdrifts. Six losses in a row. Win a game. Three losses in a row.

Mike Bibby and Toney Douglas were playing horribly. Baron Davis was still out. Iman Shumpert showed little aptitude for the point guard position. Then Carmelo, the team's leading scorer, suffered a groin injury in mid-January and looked to be out for six weeks. There was no clear ball handler or offensive catalyst on the Knicks. Still, Jeremy was the forgotten man on the bench.

Then, seemingly out of nowhere, a window of opportunity opened on Saturday, February 4. The Knicks trailed 50-42 at halftime against the New Jersey Nets. Injured star Carmelo Anthony — dressed in street clothes — pulled Coach D'Antoni aside in the locker room. He suggested that the coach play Jeremy more to see what the kid could do.

Jeremy played like he belonged in the NBA — aggressive, confident, and strong. D'Antoni left him in, and Jeremy grabbed the reins of leadership. He scored 25 points, snared five rebounds, and dished out seven assists — all career highs — leading the Knicks to a 99–92 victory.

D'Antoni liked what he saw — a real point guard running the offensive show. "You're starting Monday night," he told the second-year player.

Linsanity was about to be unleashed on an unsuspecting public.

The Rising Tide of Social Media

Since Jeremy Lin is a millennial who grew up in Silicon Valley with parents in high-tech computer jobs, technology is his friend. He's been posting his own videos on YouTube since his college days and has more than 100,000 subscribers to TheJLin7, his official YouTube channel.

He taps out tweets three or four times a week to his 600,000 followers on Twitter. His Twitter avatar shows an illustration of a white-robed Christ sitting down with a young man in a pastoral scene. There's a large duffel bag and sleeping bag beside the bench, so the young man is either a vagabond or homeless. The meaningful caption underneath the illustration: "No, I'm not talking about Twitter. I literally want you to follow me" — Jesus.

You can follow Jeremy on Twitter at @JLin7 — 7 being his old number from his Golden State Warriors days.

Chapter 14

From Couch to Center Court

On the morning of Jeremy's first NBA start against the Utah Jazz, the Knicks' webmaster made some changes to the team's website: The smiling face of youthful Jeremy Lin greeted fans on the splash page. The marketing department sent out an e-blast with "Linsanity!" in the subject line.

The Knicks were shorthanded without Amar'e Stoudemire, who was granted bereavement leave after his older brother Hazell was killed in a car crash. Carmelo Anthony tried to play but left the game after six minutes because of his nagging groin injury.

Time for Jeremy to step up.

Jeremy set the tempo with dazzling dribble drives to the basket. A nifty midair hand change for a reverse layup prompted the Knicks' home crowd to begin chanting "MVP! MVP!" They were obviously still in a celebratory mood after cheering their beloved New York Giants to a come-from-behind victory over the New England Patriots a day before in Super Bowl XLVI.

Jeremy scored a career-high 28 points against Utah, showing that his 25-point performance against the New Jersey Nets was no fluke. The fact that Jeremy orchestrated a win against a solid team with a 14-10 record attracted some notice around the league. But this was going to be a busy week for the Knicks. On Wednesday, they had a quick road trip to play the Washington Wizards, then a return home to host the Kobe-led Lakers on Friday, followed by *another* road game against Minnesota on Saturday night.

Awaiting Jeremy in the nation's capitol was John Wall. Remember him? He was the number 1 pick in the 2010 draft—and Jeremy's opposition in the final game of Summer League, the game where Jeremy played flawlessly and earned a spot with the Golden State Warriors.

On this evening, Wall was guarding Jeremy when he crossed over his dribble and blew past the defender like his sneakers were nailed to the floor. The lane opened up like the parting of the Red Sea. Instead of kissing the ball off the glass with a layup, Jeremy elevated and slammed a one-handed dunk that excited even the Wizards' home crowd.

"I think they messed up their coverage," Jeremy said after the game.[1]

Chalk up Jeremy's first double-double: 23 points and 10 assists in a 107–93 victory.

A tsunami was building. It wouldn't crest yet—that

would happen two days later when Kobe and the Lakers came to the Garden. But for now, "the fluke no longer looks so flukey," wrote Howard Beck in the *New York Times*. "The aberration is not fading away. Jeremy Lin is not regressing to the mean, whatever that mean is supposed to be."[2]

The Los Angeles Lakers rolled into the Big Apple for Friday night's game that sizzled with anticipation. Here were two storied franchises from the nation's two most populous cities squaring off, and the storyline of Jeremy vs. Kobe was too great to pass up for dozens of scribes and TV news cameras covering the Knicks beat.

After lighting the fuse on Linsanity, surely Jeremy would be put in his place by Kobe Bryant — the player Jeremy shared a birthday with — and the talented Lakers, who had won the NBA championship in two of the last three seasons. Certainly the thirty-three-year-old Lakers star had taken notice of Linsanity and would show this young man a thing or two. Surely Jeremy wasn't still sleeping on his brother's couch.

Actually, he wasn't. Now he was sleeping on the couch of his teammate Landry Fields. The night before his breakout game against the New Jersey Nets, Jeremy found himself homeless. The comfy sofa where he laid his head at his brother and sister-in-law's pad was reserved for friends who were coming over for a party.

Landry heard about Jeremy's plight and said he could crash at his place in White Plains, New York, which was close to the Knicks' training facility. Landry had a nice large brown couch in the living room. A flat-screen TV,

Hollywood filmmaker Spike Lee, a huge Knicks fan who watches nearly every game from his courtside seat, goes retro by wearing Jeremy's high school jersey during Linsanity.

refrigerator, and bathroom were steps away. What more did a recent college grad need?

Once the Knicks got hot, there was no way that Jeremy or Landry wanted to change a winning routine. Jeremy was sleeping on that couch whether he wanted to or not.

It's hard to describe how the American and global media had trained its lens on Madison Square Garden that evening, but they had. A galaxy of celebrities was on hand, including filmmaker and Knicks superfan Spike Lee, actor Ben Stiller, erstwhile wrestler and actor Dwayne "The Rock" Johnson, and New York Giants defensive hero Justin Tuck.

A lot — make that a *whole* lot — rode on the sinewy shoulders of Jeremy Shu-How Lin. He had everything to gain and just as much to lose, which is why you have to love what he did that night. All the pressure, all the hype, all the microphones, all the cameras examining every muscle twitch — and he didn't flinch.

In fact, he played out of his mind, laying down 38 points on Kobe and the Lakers. He scored at will, including tallying nine of New York's first 13 points to help the Knicks build a large lead. Jeremy nailed short jumpers, put a deft spin move on Derek Fischer to beat him to the hoop, and flung in a three-pointer from the left baseline. Kobe nearly matched him, scoring 24 of his 34 points in the second half — but Kobe left the Garden on the wrong side of a 92 – 85 Knicks victory.

Jeremy proved he was no one-week wonder in out-playing Kobe Bryant and the Lakers' team. He was being called the "Taiwanese Tebow" for the way he impacted his teammates and lifted their games—and for the forthright and earnest way he spoke about his faith.

The hype surrounding Jeremy would only grow. He was legit. The guy was for real. With the victory over the Lakers, he had four straight games with at least 20 points and seven assists.

More importantly, he had embraced the challenge of beating one of the league's top franchises in his first nationally televised game.

For a Good Cause

After Jeremy Lin outdueled Kobe Bryant on February 10 by scoring 38 points, compared to Kobe's 34, Jeremy's jersey was put up for auction on *charitybuzz.com*. The winning bidder also received four tickets to New York's home game against Atlanta on February 22 and the opportunity to meet Jeremy at the game.

The bidding began at $1,100 and ended at $42,388! All the monies went to the Garden of Dreams Foundation, which "helps dreams come true for children facing obstacles."[3] Jeremy rewarded the bidder and New York fans by scoring 17 points, handing out 9 assists, and helping the Knicks to a 99–82 victory.

Chapter 15

Lin-describable Turn of Events

With Kobe and the Lakers sent packing, New Yorkers couldn't stop talking about Jeremy Lin, and headline writers couldn't help themselves from coming up with headlines that ranged from the good to the bad to the pathetic:

- "Linsightful Lessons of Linsanity" (*Huffington Post*)
- "American-Born Linderella Is Pride of China" (NPR)
- "Just Lin Time: Knicks Phenom Saving Season" (*Chicago Tribune*)
- "Never Lin-visible, Knicks Sensation Just Needed a Chance" (*San Diego Union-Tribune*)
- "New York Knicks Legend Willis Reed Gives Ringing Lindorsement" (ESPN)

- "Linternational House of Fancakes" (*sbnation.com*)
- "Is Super Lintento All Hype or the Real Deal?" (The *Renegade Rip*)

Linsanity even invaded the Sunday morning pulpit. The Rev. John Lin, no relation to Jeremy, began his sermon at Redeemer Presbyterian on East 68th in New York by announcing that he would be teaching out of Matthew 1, the Incarnation. "Or, if you're a Knicks fan, you can call it the Lincarnation," he quipped.[1]

And that was the tip of the proverbial iceberg. Since there are twenty-seven pages of words that start with the prefix *in-* in the *American Heritage Dictionary* and an average of forty words per page, there around 1,080 possibilities to choose from if you wanted to have some fun with *Lin*.

"I didn't know you could turn *Lin* into so many things, because we've never done it before," Jeremy told Kevin Armstrong of the *New York Daily News*. "Me and my family just laugh. I guess we underestimated how creative people can be."[2]

The Knicks had a tall order following the Lakers win: hop on the team plane and fly to Minneapolis for a game the following night. Prior to tipoff, Jeremy and Landry Fields enacted a rather unique pre-game ritual that they tried out against the Washington Wizards four days earlier.

Facing each other in front of the Knicks' bench, Jeremy pretended to flip through an imaginary book that Landry was holding in his hands. Then the pair pretended to take off reading glasses, placing them into imaginary pocket protectors. The routine ended with both players simultaneously pointing to the heavens.

Okay, so it wasn't as dramatic as LeBron James tossing talcum powder into the air, but it was pretty cute. More than a few bloggers figured it had to be some sort of nerdy, bookworm faux handshake involving a Harvard grad with a former Stanford student-athlete. Actually, there was a lot more significance than that.

Landry said after Jeremy's first start, the pair wanted to come up with something since everyone was talking about the Harvard/Stanford connection. "So we wanted to go out there and do something that was lighthearted and not too serious," he said.[3]

The "book" isn't a college textbook, Landry said, but God's Word. "It's a Bible, because at the end of the day that's what we're playing for. And that's why we point up toward the sky at the end."

The Jeremy Lin Show, meanwhile, played well off Broadway. Jeremy scored 20 points against the Timberwolves, reaching the 20-point plateau for the fifth time in a row, and his free throw with 4.9 seconds left (after missing the first) gave the Knicks a 99–98 lead and capped a furious fourth-quarter comeback.

Jeremy and the Knicks team knew they had stolen a 100-98 victory in Minnesota. After Jeremy started off hot in the first half with 15 points, Ricky Rubio picked up his defensive pressure and showed why he led the league in steals. He forced Jeremy into making multiple turnovers, and Rubio even swatted away one of Jeremy's layup attempts.

But just like there are no ugly babies, there's no such thing as an ugly win. The Knicks had now captured their fifth in a row without Carmelo and Amar'e.

Seats on the Jeremy Lin bandwagon continued to fill quickly.

Whoopi Goldberg proudly donned a white number 17 Knicks jersey on the morning talkfest *The View*. Sarah Palin, during a stop in New York City, purchased a blue Linsanity T-shirt, which she held up for photographers. Donald Trump pronounced on *Access Hollywood* that Jeremy was the real deal and great for New York.

The Hoopster-in-Chief was also keeping tabs. President Barack Obama, a basketball fan who loves playing in pick-up games, said that he followed the amazing story and marveled at Jeremy's last-second shot that beat Toronto.

"It's a great story and yes, he's very impressed and fully up to speed," said White House press secretary Jay Carney. "I know he's watched Lin play already, and he had seen the highlights from last night's game," referring to how Jeremy stared down Raptors' guard Jose Calderon before draining a pull-up three-pointer for the win.[4]

Throughout February and leading up to the 2012 All-Star Game in Orlando, Jeremy continued to play at a high level. He logged a lot of minutes — 37.6 minutes over the course of the twelve games — and averaged 22.5 points per game.

If analysts had a bone to pick with Jeremy's play, it was his turnovers, committing an eye-raising 68 TOs in that twelve-game stretch, or an average of 5.6 per game.

The Knicks' seven-game win streak that marked the beginning of Linsanity came to an end against the New Orleans Hornets when Jeremy struggled to protect the ball or connect with passes. Eight first-half turnovers—and poor team shooting—put the Knicks in a hole that they couldn't overcome. Jeremy cleaned up his play in the second half, committing just one turnover, and he finished with a team-high 28 points, five assists, and four steals.

"It was just a lackluster effort on my part coming out and [being] careless with the ball," Jeremy said, owning up to his mistakes. "Nine turnovers is obviously never going to get it done from your primary ballhandler. It's on me in terms of taking care of the ball, and also the game in general."[5]

He also had a couple of "snowmen" on the stat card—8 turnovers in the memorable Toronto Raptors' victory and an ugly 8 against Miami, when a swarming defense turned up the heat in the forecourt.

A turnover can happen in a variety of ways: the ball is stolen, either through stripping it away off the dribble or intercepting a pass. A player can throw the ball out of bounds, travel with the ball, double dribble, or commit an offensive foul. Turnovers drive coaches crazy because they often result from mental mistakes and a lack of concentration.

Point guards are especially susceptible to committing turnovers, because the ball in their hands probably 70 percent of the time. Jeremy may be even more turnover prone due to his aggressive style of attacking defenses and taking the ball to the basket.

Forays into the paint are risk-reward efforts. More often than not good things happen: Jeremy either floats in a one-hander from the lane or hits one of his open teammates waiting on the wings. This type of penetration was why the Knicks won so many games prior to the All-Star break, when he took the team on a 9–3 run.

John Gabriel, the Knicks' director of pro and free agent scouting, said Jeremy's mental game was also key in turning around New York's season. "I think Jeremy has the confidence and the ability to articulate what he sees on the court and communicate it to his teammates and with the coaches. Remember, he's a rookie for the most part, yet he's shown he has natural leadership qualities, a desired attribute that can take many years to develop."

Gabriel also appreciated Jeremy's "Just win, baby" approach to the game. If that meant taking a big shot, he'd do it. If it was getting the ball to a hot teammate, consider it done. Demonstrating a true point guard mentality, Jeremy appeared happier when one of his passes led to an easy bucket for a teammate than when one of his own shots went in.

"If you're on the court with Jeremy Lin and you're open," Gabriel said, "trust that he will find you."

Jeremy was doing a great job finding his teammates, racking up double-digit assist totals in about half of the games he played. And he was about to find out what it's like to be one of the most popular players during the NBA All-Star weekend.

Get to the Point[6]

Jeremy Lin took New York by storm. As fans cheered, some sports writers tried to rank the best Knicks point guards of all time. Here's the list (Jeremy Lin earned honorable mention status, but didn't break into the top five):

1. Walt "Clyde" Frazier

Named as one of the "NBA's 50 Greatest Players," Walt led the Knicks to two NBA championships from 1967-77. He played in seven All-Star games — the same number of times he was selected on the NBA's All-Defensive team. For his career, Walt averaged nearly 19 points and dished out 6 assists a game.

2. Mark Jackson

Yes, *that* Mark Jackson, the Golden State Warriors coach who allowed Jeremy to be waived by the team. Mark had two stints with the Knicks during his seventeen-year NBA playing career. New York drafted Mark in the first round of the 1987 draft, and he rewarded the team by winning Rookie of the Year.

3. Earl Monroe

Earl joined the Knicks in 1971, and helped lead the team to two NBA championships. Called "Magic" before Magic Johnson, Earl could drive to the basket or find teammates with amazing passes.

4. Dick McGuire

Dick was the Knicks' top draft pick in 1949. Not only did he play for the Knicks, but he worked for the organization for more than fifty years. His number 15 jersey was retired in 1993.

5. Charlie Ward

In the early 1990s, Charlie was known more for his exploits on the football field than on the basketball court. He won a Heisman Trophy (which goes to college football's best player) in 1993 as quarterback for Florida State. A year later, he was quarterbacking the Knicks as their starting point guard.

Chapter 16

All-Star Onslaught

Jeremy stayed in Florida following the Miami Heat game because he was a last-second addition to the NBA's Rising Stars Challenge, which was played February 24—two nights before the All-Star game. A pool of eighteen players had been selected before Linsanity, but NBA Commissioner David Stern added Jeremy to the roster just before "coaches" Shaquille O'Neal and Charles Barkley began drafting their teams.

Shaq grabbed Jeremy after selecting monster dunker Blake Griffin of the Los Angeles Clippers as his first pick. The Rising Stars game was a super-casual affair where defense took a night off. Team Chuck beat Team Shaq 146-133 with Jeremy playing a handful of minutes and scoring one basket. After playing back-to-back games and rising to worldwide stardom, he needed a rest.

Even keeping up with media requests proved to be a nearly full-time job. Just hours before the Rising Stars Challenge tipped off, Jeremy found himself in a room crammed with more than one hundred reporters who feverishly wrote down everything he said and hoped to be able to ask a question. All of the other players had done interviews earlier in the day, but the demand to interview Jeremy was so massive that the NBA gave him his own press conference.

The fact that Jeremy was currently the only Asian-American player in the league came up over and over. He answered every question honestly, even admitting that his ethnicity may have made his path to the NBA more difficult.

"I think just being Asian-American, obviously when you look at me, I'm going to have to prove myself more so, again and again and again ..." Jeremy said. "It's something that I embrace, and it gives me a chip on my shoulder. But I'm very proud to be Asian-American, and I love it."[1]

Jeremy was also supposed to be part of the 2012 Sprite Slam Dunk contest the following night, where the NBA's best fly guys play a dunk-a-thon version of "Can You Top This?" Blake "The Quake" Griffin won the Slam Dunk event in 2011 when he leaped over a Kia Optima SX parked near the basket.

For the 2012 contest, Jeremy wasn't going to attempt any acrobatic dunks himself, but his teammate Iman Shumpert had been toying with an idea. Landry Fields would roll a large brown couch covered with a white sheet next to the basket. Jeremy would be "sleeping" underneath the cover. At the right moment, Landry would pull off the sheet and Jeremy would pop up and toss an alley-oop to Iman, who would be jumping over the couch on his way to the rim. (A riff on Blake Griffin's leap over a Kia.) Iman would throw down a monster jam and then come back and sit on the couch with Jeremy. Landry would hand Iman a can of Sprite and join his buddies on the couch.

At least, that's how they drew it up, Jeremy told TNT's Craig Sager, who interviewed Jeremy while he sat on the bench during the second half of the Rising Stars game. "We won't get a chance to do that [dunk]." Jeremy smiled, referring to a last-minute injury to Iman that caused him to pull out of the competition. "But it was an awesome and creative idea."

"Are you still sleeping on a couch?" Sager asked, referring to the brown sofa in teammate Landry Fields' apartment. During the height of Linsanity, Landry tweeted a photo of the most famous couch in the world—the brown velour sofa in his living room. ("Let the bidding begin," he joked.)

Upon hearing Sager's question, Jeremy laughed. "I have my own place," he said with a grin.

Jeremy could finally get off Landry's couch and into an apartment of his own because the Knicks stepped up and guaranteed his $762,195 salary for the rest of the year. (Actually, he only received 80 percent of that, or $609,756, because of the shortened season.) His paycheck greatly improved his bank account, but in NBA terms, it's the league minimum for second-year players.

He's the second lowest-paid Knick (Carmelo and Amar'e each make over $18 million), but expect that to change in a big way after the season when he becomes a restricted free agent. Because of the intricacies of the NBA's collective bargaining agreement and the salary cap, Jeremy figures to see an upgrade in the area of $5 million next season. That princely amount, however, will be dwarfed by what he could potentially make off the court in endorsements.

This all seems like Monopoly money when you consider that Jeremy didn't have many belongings to gather up when he moved from Landry Fields' apartment into a two-bedroom rental on the 38th floor residences at the W New York Downtown Hotel. His new place has a great view of the Statue of Liberty. The Manhattan bachelor pad was originally listed at $13,000 a month, but number 17 reportedly received a steep discount.

It's a good thing that his new abode came fully furnished because Jeremy didn't have much time to shop at HomeGoods. He was too busy trying to gel with Carmelo, Amar'e, and the rest of the Knicks in hopes of leading this Big Apple bunch deep into the NBA playoffs.

And it wouldn't be a surprise when the Knicks 2011–12 season concludes that Jeremy heads west— toward his hometown in Palo Alto and even further west to Asia.

You see, Jeremy is even more popular in his ancestral home than here in America.

Someone Had a Brain Freeze

Ben & Jerry's, the Vermont-based ice cream maker, had an error in judgment when it attempted to cash in by producing a limited-edition flavor known as "Taste the Lin-Sanity."

The ingredients: vanilla frozen yogurt with honey swirls and crumbled fortune cookies. The addition of the last ingredient left a bad taste in people's mouths, who complained of the racial overtones.

Ben & Jerry's apologized and announced that crumbled waffle cookies would replace the offending ingredient.

Chapter 17

Far East Frenzy

Jeremy's Asian heritage triggered a fan frenzy throughout Asia, but in China, the reaction was particularly intense. He was a hot topic on television sports talk shows, and his Chinese name, Lin Shuhao (the surname is said first in the Chinese culture) ranked near the top on *Baidu,* China's biggest search engine.

The timing of Jeremy's ascendency proved to be perfect for the NBA, whose largest overseas market is China. A void was created when Yao Ming, the Houston Rockets' seven-foot, six-inch center, retired in the summer of 2011 following two seasons of nagging foot and ankle problems that severely limited his play.

Jeremy appears to be the heir apparent to the Ming dynasty, and you can bet your last *yuan* that league officials will position Jeremy as the new face of the NBA's global empire. He speaks Mandarin but is not fluent, having learned the tonal language from his parents while growing up. They spoke to him in Mandarin, but he replied in English—as kids often do when they speak nothing but English outside the front door.

"I'm a lot better listening to it than I am speaking it," Jeremy said. "My Mandarin could definitely use some work."[1] He took a few classes at Harvard University to better his reading and writing skills.

After Jeremy signed his rookie contract with Golden State in the summer of 2010, he received a phone call from Yao Ming, who invited Jeremy to join the Yao Foundation in Taiwan for a goodwill trip that included helping out at children's basketball camps and playing in a charity basketball game in Taipei. Jeremy, his parents, and his two brothers jumped at the chance to be involved.

In Taipei, Jeremy scored 17 points for "Team Love," which included NBA players Brandon Jennings of the Milwaukee Bucks, Amir Johnson of the Toronto Raptors, and Hasheem Thabeet of the Memphis Grizzlies. Jeremy's paternal grandmother Lin Chu—who still lives in Taiwan—cheered on her grandson. Their competition was Team Heart, comprised of players from the Shanghai Sharks and All-Stars from the local Super Basketball League.

The Shanghai Sharks were owned by none other than ... Yao Ming. Yao and Lin bonded during the goodwill trip and have stayed in touch since. In fact during the NBA lockout, Yao attempted to sign Jeremy to play for the Shanghai Sharks. Jeremy turned down his friend because leaving American soil to play in China probably would have extinguished his dream of making his mark in the NBA.

Jeremy also received strong interest from Euroleague powerhouse Maccabi Tel Aviv in Israel—it would have been interesting for Jeremy to play a season in the Holy Land—and from Teramo Basket, a club in the Italian League.

Following Jeremy's rookie season with Golden State, he returned to Asia—twice.

He visited China for the first time in May 2011, playing in a friendly match at a middle school in Pinghu and visiting his family's ancestral home in northern China's Zhejiang province. Camera crews and photographers followed him everywhere, and he became immensely popular. Some authorities in China tried to claim him as one of their own since his maternal grandmother grew up in China, but Jeremy and his family identify themselves as Taiwanese, which creates an interesting dynamic since mainland China views the island of Taiwan as a renegade province.

While Jeremy was in China, the state news media was careful not to talk too much about Taiwan or mention his faith, which is a taboo topic because China is an atheist state. Internet searches related to Jeremy's Christian faith have been blocked in China.

Jeremy made a second visit to China a few months later, in September during the lockout. He played in a few games for the Dongguan Leopards, a team in the Chinese Basketball Association that was competing in the ABA Club Championship in Guangzhou, China.

Jeremy shakes hands with recently retired Houston Rockets center Yao Ming of China during a charity basketball game in Taipei, Taiwan. Jeremy scored 17 points while playing with other NBA players on "Team Love."

Jeremy was named the MVP, and once again, he was big news in the Chinese media.

Jeremy didn't mind the media attention back then, but once Linsanity went global in February 2012 he worried about his family, especially his eighty-five-year-old grandmother. Paparazzi camped out at Lin Chu's door and started following her everywhere. At first she tried to be helpful, even releasing baby photos of Jeremy and doing interviews.

NBA Minority

The NBA estimates that 300 million people in China play basketball. (As a reference, 311 million people *live* in the United States.) Despite the huge numbers of Chinese who play basketball, only a handful have risen to the game's highest level.

Yao Ming

Yao Ming wasn't the tallest player to ever play in the NBA — seven-foot, seven-inch Manute Bol and Gheorghe Muresan share that distinction — but he is almost half a foot taller than Pau Gasol, Dirk Nowitzki, and Shaquille O'Neal. Throughout his eight-year, injury-plagued career with the Houston Rockets, he was the face of basketball in Asia. When Yao was healthy, he was one of the most dominant centers in the league with a career average of 19 points and 9.2 rebounds a game.

Yi Jianlian

During the 2011-12 season, Yi Jianlian played forward for the Dallas Mavericks. The seven-footer has bounced between four teams in his five-year NBA career. His best season came in 2008-09 when he averaged 12 points a game for the New Jersey Nets.

Sun Yue

This six-foot, nine-inch guard saw limited time for the Los Angeles Lakers in six games during the 2008–09 season. He was the fifth Chinese athlete to play in the NBA.

Mengke Bateer

Mengke Bateer played from 2001–2003 in the NBA. The six-foot, eleven-inch center enjoyed his best season with the Denver Nuggets where he averaged 5.1 points a game in 2001–02.

Wang Zhizhi

The Dallas Mavericks drafted the seven-foot center in the second round of the 1999 NBA draft. Wang Zhizhi joined the Mavs in 2000, making him the first Chinese player to play in the NBA. He played seven years for three different teams. His best seasons were his first two in Dallas, where he averaged over five points a game.

"I don't know too much about basketball ..." she admitted. "I only know when Jeremy puts the ball in the basket he has done a good thing."[2]

But soon the media blitz became too much and Jeremy asked reporters to give his family space.

The pressures of fame can be tough — even on extended family — so it's not a bad idea to pray that Jeremy will stand strong.

Chapter 18

A Prayer Request from and for Jeremy

Each night before the New York Knicks play at Madison Square Garden, there's a mini church service for the players led by the Rev. John Love. He drives nearly two hundred miles from Baltimore, where he's been the youth pastor at the Greater Grace World Outreach since 1983. Pastor Love has served faithfully—and rolled off more than 400,000 miles—as the Knicks' chaplain for twenty-five years.

Pastor Love keeps a low profile, which could be said for the entire NBA chaplaincy program. Many basketball fans don't realize that a chapel service is held before every NBA game—regular season and playoffs—with players from *both* teams welcome to attend.

This open invitation makes pro basketball different from other major sports, where players from opposing teams attend separate chapel services.

One hour before tip-off, the home-team chaplain invites players from both teams to attend a short service. Attendance is voluntary. Sometimes they sing a worship song. Then the chaplain speaks for ten or fifteen minutes, sharing Scripture and teaching from the Bible. The basic goal is to equip players to live lives that glorify God and to encourage them to remain strong in the face of temptation.

At the end, players sometimes share a prayer request, or ask a question about the chaplain's message. Discussions must move quickly, since the players must get on the court to warm up for the game.

Less than an hour after these athletes sit and pray together, the referee tosses the ball into the air and they try to outplay each other on the court.

When Jeremy first joined Golden State, he was surprised how quickly players could go from soft-heartedly worshiping God to playing intense basketball and executing hard fouls. At the same time, he really enjoyed chapel.

"It's actually really cool to see believers from other teams," Jeremy said. "A lot of NBA players came [to the chapels]. I enjoyed that a lot."

On January 27, 2012, one week before the launch of Linsanity, Jeremy walked down the hallway from his dressing room in Miami's American Airlines Arena to participate in the pregame chapel. Just a handful of players from both teams joined him, including Udonis Haslem, a Miami Heat forward and a regular at these twenty-minute assemblies.

After the chaplain shared his devotional, he asked if there were any prayer requests.

Jeremy raised his hand. "That I don't get cut again."[1]

At that point, his NBA career was tenuous. Jeremy didn't play much, and his chance to shine against the New Jersey Nets was still in the future.

God answered that prayer in a mighty way, which should make the NBA glad. Because if you think about it, Jeremy may have saved the 2011–12 regular season.

During the darkest days of the lockout in November 2011, the American public didn't seem to care. They were caught up in Tebowmania. *No one pays attention to the NBA until the playoffs start, right?*

Then Jeremy came along. He made professional basketball exciting again. No matter what a person's team allegiance may have been, everyone pulled for him.

Jeremy's story was one for the ages, a feel-good tale that resonated with basketball fans and even those who didn't pay much attention to the sport. What Jeremy accomplished in a short time goes deeper than the fact that he was the first Taiwanese-American in the NBA.

Stories like Jeremy's aren't supposed to happen. It's really unfathomable that an undrafted prospect—who logged just a few minutes in the NBA—could come roaring off the bench and turn around a storied franchise in the media mecca of New York City. But it did happen, so people jumped to their feet to cheer the underdog who was told he wasn't good enough.

Even *before* Linsanity, things were a little crazy for Jeremy. During the 2011 summer, "church tourists" dropped by the Chinese Church in Christ to hound Jeremy for autographs and to have their picture taken with him. Things got to the point where Pastor Stephen Chen issued a statement from the pulpit informing everyone that Jeremy would not sign autographs or have pictures taken with him, and to please not bother him.

Like everyone else, Pastor Chen didn't foresee Linsanity. "I don't know if anybody could have seen it coming, that he would become essentially a global icon overnight."

The New York media tracked down the Mountain View pastor rather quickly. They wanted to know what role Jeremy's faith played in his basketball and how his faith had helped him through numerous disappointments. Pastor Chen felt this line of questioning was trying to make God out as a heavenly ATM machine—that if you pray hard enough, believe hard enough, then God will bless you and give you what you want.

Pastor Chen patiently explained that things don't work that way. He pointed out that Jeremy's goal was obedience and true worship. Sure, Jeremy turned to God and his Word in the hard times. Jeremy often cited Romans 5:3-5 as his favorite verses: "We also rejoice in our sufferings, because we know that suffering produces perseverance; perseverance, character; and character, hope. And hope does not disappoint us." Jeremy's success wasn't something he'd earned solely on his own ability and willpower, it happened through God's grace and for a reason.

So what has Jeremy Lin wrought? What will the future bring?

Who knows what the answers are—but that's the beauty of sport and the uncertainty of life. You never know what will happen.

As *Linspired* went to press, the Jeremy Lin story continued to fascinate hundreds of millions of people around the world. People genuinely *liked* him, and well they should. They recognized that Jeremy was an uncommon young man with uncommon leadership skills, extraordinary athletic gifts, and an authentic faith in Christ.

"I want to be able to sit back when I'm done with my career and say that I gave everything I could and that I did it for God's glory," Jeremy said. "When I say do it for God's glory, there's a lot of things I want to do off the court in terms of the platform of an NBA player to be able to impact the world. I'm thankful for the platform, but I don't want people to lose sight of the team, because without the team, I'm nothing."[2]

It all happened so fast, arriving at the busy intersection where sport, religion, fame, and pop culture meet.

Pray for Jeremy Lin as he looks both ways and crosses the street.

And pray that he continues to hold the Lord's hand.

Linsanity versus Tebowmania

Have you noticed that the two most talked-about athletes in the world are two Christians named Jeremy Lin and Tim Tebow?

These young men don't hide the fact that they're dedicated followers of Christ without "imposing" their faith in preachy, heavy-handed ways. They live honest lives, remain humble about their accomplishments, and give glory to God.

"They're two of the biggest names in American sports — and now, they're friends," declared the lead sentence in a February 23, 2012, *People* magazine story.[3] Adrian Tam, Jeremy's spiritual mentor at the Asian-American Christian Fellowship at Harvard, was the one who dished. "They've spoken over the telephone," Tam said. "Jeremy's been a fan of Tebow for a while, but only recently were they able to connect. His comment to me was that Tim is a really great guy and that he's very inspired by him."

Jeremy and Tim finally got to meet at the ESPY Awards in Los Angeles in July 2012. Jeremy received a trophy for "Best Breakthrough Athlete," and Tim won for "Best Moment." Tim Tebow was one of Jeremy's award presenters (with actress Jessica Biel). Afterward, Tim and Jeremy posed in comical photos with Jessica — Jeremy wearing a king's crown and gigantic shades and Tim sporting a fake moustache and black-rimmed glasses — which Jeremy posted on his Twitter account. Let's hope they get a chance to hang out longer than a backstage grip-and-grin.

Chapter 19

Back to the Future

Three weeks after the 2012 NBA All-Star game, two things derailed the runaway locomotive known as Linsanity:

1. Knicks' head coach Mike D'Antoni quit.
2. Jeremy's season ended with knee surgery.

Jeremy was upset after D'Antoni left. After all, Mike D'Antoni had saved Jeremy's career. And now his coach was gone.

Meanwhile, Jeremy continued to play a lot as the team won six of the next seven games. But his chronically sore knee couldn't take it. That's when Jeremy found out he had a partially torn meniscus. Doctors told Jeremy he had to stop playing. He needed arthroscopic knee surgery, and he would miss at least six weeks of the season. At best, he could be back for the opening round of the playoffs.

In the hospital, Jeremy tweeted a picture of himself, droopy-eyed in his hospital bed. "Praise God for a successful surgery ... road to recovery! Lets goo."

Jeremy faded off the sports pages, and a Linsanity backlash set in. It may have started with the magazine *Sports Illustrated*, which asked: "Are we done with Jeremy Lin?" Then the *New York Post* published a picture of a marble tombstone with the following inscription:

R.I.P.
LINSANITY
Briefly Beloved Broadway Smash Hit
February 4, 2012
to
March 14, 2012

Jeremy may have had an inkling that his days as a New York Knick were numbered.

So what was next for Jeremy? It was no surprise that team doctors didn't clear Jeremy to play during the first round of the NBA playoffs between the Knicks and the Miami Heat. And his situation with the Knicks was up in the air. He was a restricted free agent, meaning other teams could make him an offer and the Knicks could try to match it or not.

But did the Knicks want Jeremy? Logically, yes. Jeremy made Madison Square Garden an exciting place to watch basketball again. Spike Lee, a filmmaker who has courtside seats, said Linsanity was the loudest he'd ever heard the stadium. Jeremy's playing got people to buy tickets, lifted TV ratings, and sold a ton of merchandise. Jeremy gave the Knicks street cred.

Knicks' head coach Mike Woodson made a trip out to Los Angeles in late June to visit Carmelo Anthony, Tyson Chandler, and Jeremy Lin, who was back in his old bedroom at his parents' Palo Alto home for the summer. Jeremy met his coach and teammates, and it was like old times. Woodson confirmed that Jeremy was his point guard and that the Knicks were going places. They wanted Jeremy in the mix.

Jeremy left the dinner on a high.

At first, no other teams made an offer to Jeremy. Then Jeremy's agent was told by the Knicks, *Oh, by the way, we're also looking at other point guards.* It didn't make sense, so Jeremy's agent called other teams to see if they wanted to make an offer too. Jeremy was open to offers.

One of the teams was the Houston Rockets — the last team to waive Jeremy before the Knicks rescued him from obscurity. During Linsanity, Rockets' general manager Daryl Morey, had tweeted: "We should have kept @JLin7. Did not know he was this good. Anyone who says they knew misleading U."

Morey said how sorry they were they cut Jeremy, that it was all a big mistake, and it never should have happened. Then he made a big offer — three years and $19 million.

We'll match that, the Knicks said.

This was like high-stakes poker. Morey threw more chips into the pile — three years and $25 million. All Jeremy and his agent could do was wait to see what the Knicks would do.

A few days later, Jeremy was surfing the Web when a

headline caught his eye: *Knicks acquire Felton in sign-and-trade with Blazers.*[1] Felton was a free agent point guard from the Portland Trail Blazers. The decision to trade for Felton meant only one thing to Jeremy. He was no longer a New York Knick; they were going with someone else since the team would not match Houston's offer.

Jeremy knew better than anyone else that something special had happened with the rise of Linsanity. He wanted to stay in New York. But this time the ball wasn't in his hands. Someone else was directing traffic on the court. His days of playing basketball as a New York Knick were over. It really *was* Linsanity, R.I.P.

Daryl Morey tweeted a personal message to Jeremy and all Rockets fans: "Welcome to Houston @Jlin7! We plan to hang on this time."

A few weeks after Jeremy signed his new contract with the Houston Rockets, he gave an interview to the *San Jose Mercury News*. The reporter asked Jeremy if all the Linsanity craziness went to his head.

"If I'm being honest, in some ways, yes," he replied. "I fought it every day. But I think subconsciously it had its effect, everyone catering to you."

Jeremy wouldn't be human if he wasn't aware of what was happening around him on the island of Manhattan during February 2012. The number of words written about him—in the traditional news, on blogs, and via Twitter and Facebook—was absolutely mind-boggling.

And then came the switch—people saying Jeremy was overrated.

"People were saying only good things for so long

that when people said negative stuff, it was like, 'Whoa, what's going on?'" Jeremy said to Thompson, who wrote this:

> After Lin signed a three-year, $25 million contract with the Houston Rockets, a lot of negative things were said. He's selfish. He's all about the money. His ego is out of control. And, to top it off, many deemed him a basketball fluke who already has maxed out his potential.
>
> But Lin is happy. He said he is thankful for his time in New York with the Knicks, the ride of a lifetime. He said he is eager about his future in Houston and the possibilities with his new team. And he doesn't seem too concerned with repairing his image or proving himself right. He said too much is going well to be worried about the negative.[2]

Now a new chapter was starting in Texas. The first thing Jeremy did when he arrived in Houston was regain his old Number 7 jersey number.

The Rockets didn't have a great 2011–12 season (34–32), so they went through major changes during the offseason. The team let five of their top six scorers go, and four of the replacements were rookies. Let's just say that Jeremy wasn't dribbling into the greatest basketball situation.

But that all changed with a blockbuster deal as the 2012–13 season began — when the Rockets and Oklahoma City Thunder traded seven players and three draft picks. The big catch for the Rockets was the NBA's Sixth Man of the Year for the 2011–12 season: James

Harden, an elite ballplayer who is likely to be among the top ten scorers in the NBA now that he's getting a lot more minutes with the Rockets.

Suddenly, with Harden and Lin, the Rockets were sporting one of the most exciting lineups. Harden wears a long, Moses-length beard, a good indication that Jeremy and James are spiritually in sync as well.

"I just want to thank God for everything he has done in my life," Harden tweeted after he scored 37 points in his debut game with the Rockets. "I really am a believer. All glory to the man above."[3] Harden has been photographed wearing the same **In Jesus' Name I Play** rubber wristbands as Jeremy.

With Harden scoring buckets by the bushel and Jeremy doing the same (Jeremy scored 38 points in their December 10, 2012, game against the San Antonio Spurs[4]), the Jeremy Lin Show is on again, at least for the foreseeable future.

About the Authors

Mike Yorkey, the author or co-author of more than seventy books, has written about sports all his life for a variety of national sports publications and book publishers. He has collaborated with Cleveland Browns quarterback Colt McCoy and his father, Brad, in *Growing Up Colt*; San Francisco Giants pitcher Dave Dravecky (*Called Up* and *Play Ball*), tennis stars Michael Chang (*Holding Serve*) and Betsy McCormack (*In His Court*), and San Diego Chargers placekicker Rolf Benirschke (*Alive & Kicking*).

His most recent sports book is *Playing with Purpose: Inside the Lives and Faith of the Major League's Top Players* (with Jesse Florea and Joshua Cooley), which released with the start of the 2012 baseball season. He also authored *Playing with Purpose: Inside the Lives and Faith of Top NBA Stars* in 2011 and *Playing with Purpose: Inside the Lives and Faith of the NFL's Top New Quarterbacks — Sam Bradford, Colt McCoy, and Tim Tebow* in 2010.

Yorkey, who graduated from the University of Oregon's School of Journalism, is a former editor of *Focus on the Family* magazine who has also written for sports magazines such as *Skiing, Tennis*, and *Breakaway*. He is also a novelist, and his latest fiction effort is *Chasing Mona Lisa*, a World War II thriller he co-authored with Tricia Goyer.

He and his wife, Nicole, are the parents of two adult children, Andrea and Patrick. They make their home in Encinitas, California. His website is *www.mikeyorkey.com*.

Jesse Florea has covered high school sports and written about professional athletes for more than twenty-five years. He has written or co-written a dozen books, including the recently released *Playing with Purpose: Inside the Lives and Faith of the Major League's Top Players* (with Mike Yorkey and Joshua Cooley) and *The One-Year Devos for Kids Who Love Sports.* Many of his sports stories appear in *Focus on the Family Clubhouse* (for boys and girls ages eight to twelve), a magazine that he's been the editor of for fifteen years. During his eighteen-year career at Focus on the Family, he's also worked as the editor of *Clubhouse Jr.* magazine (for children three to seven), associate editor of *Breakaway* magazine (teen boys) and edited the parenting edition of *Focus on the Family* magazine. He earned bachelor and master's degrees in communications from Wheaton College.

He lives with his wife, Stephanie, and two teenagers, Nate and Amber, in Colorado Springs.

Endnotes*

Chapter 1

1. Robert Klemko, " 'Linsanity' Crosses Border as Knicks Beat Raptors," *USA Today,* February 15, 2012, and available at http://www.usatoday.com/sports/basketball/nba/story/2012-02-14/Linsanity-crosses-border-as-Knicks-beat-Raptors/53098444/1

2. Ibid.

3. Mason Levinson and Scott Soshnick, "Jeremy Lin Files Patent Office Request to Trademark 'Linsanity,' " *Bloomberg Businessweek,* February 23, 2012, and available at http://www.businessweek.com/news/2012-02-23/jeremy-lin-files-patent-office-request-to-trademark-linsanity-.html

Chapter 2

1. Peter May, "Harvard prodigy Jeremy Lin Returns," ESPNBoston.com, March 3, 2012, and available at http://espn.go.com/boston/nba/story/_id/7643951/harvard-prodigy-jeremy-lin-returns-new-york-knicks-face-boston-celtics

2. Erik Matuszewski, "Jeremy Lin Has Opponents Targeting Knicks as Heat's LeBron James Awaits," *Bloomberg Businessweek,* February 23, 2012, and available at http://www.bloomberg.com/news/2012-02-23/jeremy-lin-has-opponents-targeting-knicks-as-heat-s-lebron-james-awaits.html

* All quotations not sourced to a specific publication come from personal interviews between Mike Yorkey and Jeremy Lin, Pastor Stephen Chen, Adrian Tam, Alek Blankenau, Jeff Ryan, Michael Chang, and John Gabriel.

Chapter 3

1. "Lin Book Soon, Taiwan School Show Knicks Games," *USAToday.com,* February 22, 2012, and available at http://www.usatoday.com/sports/basketball/nba/story/2012-02-22/Lin-book-soon-Taiwan-schools-show-Knicks-games/53204814/1

Chapter 4

1. Arash Ghadishah, "Jeremy Lin's High-School Coach Recalls a Star on the Rise," *The Daily Beast,* February 18, 2012, and available at http://www.thedailybeast.com/articles/2012/02/18/jeremy-lin-s-high-school-coach-recalls-a-star-on-the-rise.html

Chapter 5

1. Sean Gregory, "Harvard's Hoops Star Is Asian. Why's That a Problem?" *Time* magazine, December 31, 2009, and available at http://www.time.com/time/magazine/article/0,9171,1953708,00.html

2. Tim Keown, "Jeremy Lin's HS Coach Is Surprised, Too," ESPN.com, February 14, 2012, and available at http://espn.go.com/espn/commentary/story/_/id/7574452/jeremy-lin-high-school-coach-surprised-too

3. Eric Branch, "Jeremy Lin's Rise From Ordinary Guy to Sensation," the *San Francisco Chronicle,* February 23, 2012, and available at http://www.sfgate.com/cgi-bin/article.cgi?f=/c/a/2012/02/23/MN2N1NB2OL.DTL

4. Ibid.

Chapter 6

1. Ghadishah, "Jeremy Lin's High-School Coach Recalls a Star on the Rise."

2. Chuck Culpepper, "An All-Around Talent, Obscured by His Pedigree," *The New York Times*, September 14, 2010, and

available at http://www.nytimes.com/2010/09/15/sports/
basketball/15nba.html

3. Myrna Blyth, "Meet Jeremy Lin's Tiger Mom," thirdage.
   com, February 17, 2012, and available at http://www.
   thirdage.com/celebrities/jeremy-lins-tiger-mother

Chapter 7

1. Pablo S. Torre, "From Couch to Clutch," *Sports Illustrated,*
   February 20, 2012, and available at http://sportsillustrated.
   cnn.com/vault/article/magazine/MAG1194909/index.htm

2. Chris Dortch, "Harvard Was Perfect Place for Lin to Hone
   Guard Skills," nba.com, February 17, 2012, and available at
   http://www.nba.com/2012/news/features/chris_dortch/
   02/17/lin-college-break/index.html

3. "Jeremy Lin: Taking Harvard Basketball to New Levels,"
   published in InterVarsity's Spiritual Journeys page, March
   12, 2010, and available at http://www.intervarsity.org/
   studentsoul/item/jeremy-lin

4. Ibid.

Chapter 8

1. "Jeremy Lin: Taking Harvard Basketball to New Levels."

2. Commentator quotes taken from "What They're Saying
   About Harvard Basketball and Jeremy," Harvard sports
   website, December 11, 2009, and available at http://www.
   gocrimson.com/sports/mbkb/2009-10/releases/091210_
   MBB_Quotes

3. Pablo S. Torre, "Harvard School of Basketball," *Sports
   Illustrated*, February 1, 2010, and available at http://
   sportsillustrated.cnn.com/vault/article/magazine/
   MAG1165302/1/index.html

4. Poor Man's Commish, "Jeremy Lin: The New Steve Nash,
   making Asian-American History Tonight in Santa Clara, of
   all places," goldenstateofmind.com, January 4, 2010, and

available at http://www.goldenstateofmind.com/2010/1/4/
1232730/jeremy-lin-the-new-steve-nash

Chapter 9

1. Ed Welland, "NBA Draft Preview 2010: Jeremy Lin, G Harvard," hoopsanalyst.com, and available at http://hoopsanalyst.com/blog/?p=487
2. Tim Kawakami, "Lacob Interview, Part 3: On Jeremy Lin, Ellison, Larry Riley, Bold Moves, and Poker," Talking Points website, August 17, 2010, and available at http://blogs.mercurynews.com/kawakami/2010/08/17/lacob-interview-part-3-on-jeremy-lin-ellison-larry-riley-bold-moves-and-poker/

Chapter 10

1. Samantha Gilman, "Sustaining Faith," *World* magazine, February 16, 2012, and available at http://www.worldmag.com/webextra/19193
2. Ibid.
3. Ibid.
4. Dan Duggan, "Jeremy Lin's Teammates Are Enjoying 'Linsanity' as Much as Anyone," *Boston Herald*, February 17, 2012, and available at http://www.bostonherald.com/blogs/sports/oncampus/?p=415

Chapter 12

1. Training schedule information taken from Keown, "Jeremy Lin's HS Coach Is Surprised, Too."
2. Daniel Brown, "Bay Area Trainers Helped Make Knicks Guard Jeremy Lin Better, Stronger, Faster," *Silicon Valley Mercury News*, February 23, 2012, and available at http://www.mercurynews.com/top-stories/ci_20033514
3. Marcus Thompson II, "Exclusive: Jeremy Lin Says Faith in God Triggered 'Lin-Sanity,'" *Silicon Valley Mercury News*,

February 13, 2012, and available at http://www.
mercurynews.com/jeremy-lin/ci_19954877

4. Tom Van Riper, "Lin Could Have Added $10 Million to
Warriors Value," *Forbes*, February 14, 2012, and available at
http://www.forbes.com/sites/tomvanriper/2012/02/14/
lin-could-have-added-10-million-to-warriors-value/

Chapter 13

1. Michael Moraitis, "New York Knicks: Jeremy Lin Isn't the
Only Right Move GM Glen Grunwald Has Made,"
bleacherreport.com, February 22, 2012, and available at
http://bleacherreport.com/articles/1076278-new-york-
knicks-jeremy-lin-isnt-the-only-right-move-gm-glen-grunwald-
has-made

2. Sean Brennan, Harvard grad Jeremy Lin claimed off waivers
by NY Knicks; Asian-American guard offers back court
insurance *New York Daily News*, December 27, 2011, and
available at http://www.nydailynews.com/sports/
basketball/knicks/harvard-grad-jeremy-lin-claimed-waivers-
ny-knicks-asian-american-guard-offers-backcourt-insurance-
article-1.997304

3. Ibid.

4. Erik Qualman, "Jeremy Lin: Lin-Sanity Hits Twitter @
JLin7," socialnomics.com, February 15, 2012, and available
at http://www.socialnomics.net/2012/02/15/jeremy-lin-lin-
sanity-hits-twitter-jlin7/

5. Jeff Zillgitt, "Jeremy Lin Humbled, Humorous During
All-Star Weekend," *USA Today*, February 25, 2012, and
available at http://www.usatoday.com/sports/basketball/
nba/knicks/story/2012-02-25/jermey-lin-all-star-
weekend/53244342/1

6. Thompson II, "Exclusive: Jeremy Lin Says Faith in God
Triggered 'Lin-Sanity.'"

Chapter 14

1. Frank Isola, "Jeremy Lin leads NY Knicks to another victory with 23 points, 10 assists in 107–93 win over John Wall and Wizards," *New York Daily News*, February 9, 2012, and available at http://www.nydailynews.com/sports/basketball/knicks/jeremy-lin-leads-ny-knicks-victory-23-points-10-assists-107-93-win-john-wall-wizards-article-1.1019541

2. Howard Beck, "Lin Leads Again as Knicks Win 3rd in a Row," *The New York Times*, February 8, 2012, and available at http://www.nytimes.com/2012/02/09/sports/basketball/jeremy-lin-leads-knicks-again-107-93-over-wizards.html?scp=1&sq=lin-leads-again-as-knicks-win-3rd-in-a-row

3. Mason Levinson, "Jeremy Lin's Knicks Jersey From Lakers Win Auctions for $42,388," *Bloomberg Businessweek,* February 22, 2012, and available at http://www.businessweek.com/news/2012-02-22/jeremy-lin-s-knicks-jersey-from-lakers-win-auctions-for-42-388.html

Chapter 15

1. Tim Stelloh and Noah Rosenberg, "From the Pulpit and in the Pew, the Knicks' Lin Is a Welcome Inspiration," The *New York Times*, February 12, 2012, and available at http://www.nytimes.com/2012/02/13/sports/basketball/from-the-pulpit-and-in-the-pew-the-knicks-lin-is-a-welcome-inspiration.html

2. Kevin Armstrong, "Jeremy Lin: The True Hollywood Story of the Knick Sensation Who's Taken Over New York In Less Than a Week," *New York Daily News*, February 11, 2012, and available at http://www.nydailynews.com/sports/basketball/knicks/jeremy-lin-true-hollywood-story-knick-sensation-york-a-week-article-1.1021119

3. "Jeremy Lin's Religious Pregame Ritual," thestar.com, February 13, 2012, and available at http://www.thestar.com/sports/basketball/nba/article/1130493--video-jeremy-lin-s-religious-pregame-ritual

4. David Nakamura, "President Obama Catches Jeremy Lin Fever After Watching 'Lin-sanity' Highlights," *Washington Post,* February 15, 2012, and available at http://www.washingtonpost.com/blogs/44/post/president-obama-catches-jeremy-lin-fever-after-watching-lin-sanity-highlights/2012/02/15/gIQA1oIxFR_blog.html

5. Jeff Zillgitt, "Jeremy Lin Scores 26, but Hornets Snap Knicks' Win Streak," *USA Today*, February 16, 2012, and available at http://www.usatoday.com/sports/basketball/nba/story/2012-02-17/Jeremy-Lin-scores-26-but-Knicks-streak-ends/53138060/1

6. List taken from Josh Benjamin, "Ranking the Best Knicks Point Guards in Franchise History," bleacherreport.com, March 1, 2012, and available at http://bleacherreport.com/articles/1086355-ranking-the-best-knicks-point-guards-in-franchise-history/page/2

Chapter 16

1. Howard Beck, "Lin's New Challenge: Media Onslaught at All-Star Weekend," *The New York Times,* February 24, 2012, and available at http://www.nytimes.com/2012/02/25/sports/basketball/lins-new-challenge-media-onslaught-at-all-star-weekend.html

Chapter 17

1. Irv Soonachan, "Point of Attention: Rookie Jeremy Lin Has Proven He Can Play in the NBA," slamonline.com, April 5, 2011, and available at http://www.slamonline.com/online/nba/2011/04/point-of-attention/

2. Keith Bradsher, "An Odd Game a Grandmother Can Appreciate," *The New York Times,* February 15, 2012, and available at http://www.nytimes.com/2012/02/16/sports/basketball/jeremy-lins-grandmother-watches-along-with-taiwan.html

Chapter 18

1. Mike Vaccaro, "Lin Had Prayer Answered After First Knicks-Heat Matchup," *New York Post*, February 23, 2012, and available at http://www.nypost.com/p/sports/knicks/lin_goes_from_pray_to_prey_5t1JmO0e1J5czHN10tMiLN

2. Dan Duggan, "Always Believe-Lin," *Boston Herald*, February 17, 2012, and available at http://bostonherald.com/sports/basketball/other_nba/view/20220217always_believe-lin_jeremy_lins_miracle_rise_a_story_of_faith_and_persistence

3. Kristen Mascia, "Tim Tebow & Jeremy Lin Connect Over Faith," *People* magazine, February 23, 2012, and available at http://www.people.com/people/article/0,,20572929,00.html

Chapter 19: Back to the Future

1. Matt Moore, "Knicks Acquire Felton in Sign-and-Trade with Blazers," CBS Sports.com, July 14, 2012, www.cbssports.com/nba/blog/eye-on-basketball/19587022 (accessed November 26, 2012).

2. Marcus Thompson II, "Jeremy Lin Exclusive: I Will Always Have Haters," *San Jose Mercury News*, July 23, 2012.

3. Quoted in Christine Thomasos, "James Harden Wanted Time to Pray before Leaving OKC," *Christian Post*, November 7, 2012, www.christianpost.com/news/james-harden-wanted-time-to-pray-before-leaving-okc-84599/ (accessed November 26, 2012).

4. Adi Joseph, "Linsanity: Jeremy Lin Finally Breaks Out for Houston Rockets," *USA Today,* December 11, 2012, www.usatoday.com/story/sports/nba/rockets/2012/12/11/

Defender of Faith:
The Mike Fisher Story

Kim Washburn

Mike Fisher knows the true meaning of a power play.

As a veteran of the National
Hockey League, Mike Fisher has
a lot to be proud of. He plays for
the Nashville Predators, was an
alternate captain for the Ottawa
Senators, competed in the
Stanley Cup finals, and has been
nominated for the Selke Trophy
as the best defensive forward in
the league. But it's not just his

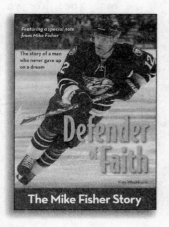

guts, grit, and talent that have brought him success. His power
comes from the top—he puts his faith in Christ first and has
demonstrated his love for God both on and off the ice.

Available in stores and online!

We want to hear from you. Please send your comments about this book to us in care of zreview@zondervan.com. Thank you.

ZONDERVAN.com/
AUTHORTRACKER
follow your favorite authors